ADVANCE COPY
[This is the Pre-Release Version of The Newest Secret.]

Thank you for reading this Review Copy.
You may write your review at

http://www.amazon.com/The-Newest-Secret-
Introduction-Planning/dp/0615834817/ref=sr_1_1?ie
=UTF8&qid=1373657209&sr=8-1&keywords=book
s+the+newest+secret+deborah+s+nelson

Free BONUS!

Go to
http://authoryourdreams.com/111-positive-quotes-to-keep-your-dreams-alive/ for your free Weekly Dreams Quotes ($37 value!)

Scan here to immediately go to the free bonus page.

Living Her Best Life.

"I am in Kampala Uganda serving the management and staff as they premier the reality show loosely based on The Apprentice (Donald Trump). As I stand in the glimmering lights of TV Cameras, members of the press, celebrities and leaders of the Uganda Parliament, I reflect on how nice it is to have made my dreams a reality.

Not long ago, Deborah S. Nelson gifted me with her Course Author Your Dreams based on the Newest Secret and the Author Your Dreams companion workbook. I had nurtured a dream to for most of my adult life to "Come Home to Africa."

Deborah's loving but firm coaching, the homework assignments, the inner work and the resulting clarity offered me all the support I needed to start on a magnificent journey of manifesting my dreams and living life with ease and grace.

Deborah S. Nelson is in a league of her own, offering expertise at a level of excellence with wisdom, love and compassion in service to the realization of dreams for hundreds of thousands."

[After publishing her vision book, Audrey spent 17 months in East Africa where she spoke to thousands of university and high school students. She runs a successful consulting business and is launching a nationwide grassroots movement in early 2014.]

—Audrey Addison Williams,
CEO, *Inspire Africa Academy*
(Kampala, East Africa)

Dream Catcher Tool.

Great Tool for establishing dreams suitable for junior high students through college and adult seekers. Positive affirmations and simple step by step activities make this a must have tool for those ready to plan for future, write a practical life plan, or even write a book!

—Dr. Deborah De Vries,
School Trustee and
College Instructor
(Ventura, CA)

Positively Transform Lives.

This is a serious "self-help" formula that I believe could actually make a reader's dreams come true, IF they seriously followed the instructions of the author. In my opinion, this book often reads like *The Power of Now* or *A Course in Miracles*—which one should consider as a "good thing." After all, *The Power of Now* and *A Course in Miracles* did positively transform thousands of lives!

—Amelia A. Painter,
Author (Fostoria, IA USA)

A Life-Changing Course!

Deborah S. Nelson's course, *Author Your Book*, which uses the *Author Your Reality Text* along with the *Author Your Book Workbook*, was fantastic! The material was easy and straightforward. There is a 10 step 'author your reality' process she takes you through which can be applied to manifesting any dream, I suppose. However, my dream was to become an author. I have 5 books in the making that I've never completed. Through this course I finally finished and published my very first book! What a rush. What a dream come true. I now have many of the skills, the courage and the inspiration to continue onward and upward! I took this class in person, however you can do it from your home. Everyone in her class published their own book in 8 weeks. I give a big two thumbs up for this course work. Get both the text and the workbook, as they're a set.

—Cindy M. White, Author,
The Ripple Effect Game (Santa Barbara, CA)

The Whole Picture.

I took Deborah's *Author Your Book* Course. I was at a stage in my book where I hit the wall. I met with Deborah privately who brainstormed with me on the message I was trying to convey. I did not have a solid title yet and Deborah helped me to see how important that was. Once I got the right title, the whole book came together. Her insight, guidance and ability to see the whole picture on! Thanks, Deborah.

—Eve Briere, Founder,
Successful Organizing Solutions,
Author, 31 Days, 31 Spaces

Easy Road to Goal Achievement.

Author Your Reality, when used with its Workbook, truly helps the reader determine their dreams (goals), and list them–which is very important. Then you pick one and and ride it to fruition in a wonderful manner. I was pleasantly surprised, since I don't think of myself as dreamer. Well done, Deborah.

—Larry Melby,
(Carpenteria, CA)

Get This Book Series!

For a lot of us, it's not that we don't have dreams. Life gets busy and all we get to do is what needs to be done. This book is a call to action to get started with bringing your dreams to reality. *Author Your Reality* helps you define your dream and get you started with actually making the steps to fulfill that dream. Want to get started working on your dream? Get this book!

—Peter Kahuria
(OK, USA)

Wisdom in a Little Book.

The author distills and simplifies centuries of wisdom in this little easy to read guidebook for setting & accomplishing life goals. Well worth owning a copy. You'll likely keep it as a long-term guidebook to your universe.

—Carol Stall
(Austin, TX)

Invest in Yourself.

Be ready to conquer the fear of failure, as that word is not in Ms. Nelson's vocabulary. She will help you to look at all facets of your life, find your dream, separate the truth from fantasy and inspire you to take action to make your own dream come true. Don't buy the book – invest in yourself by investing in this book that will turn your Dreams to Reality. I did!

—Bill Hood Books,
Bill Hood (Austin, TX)

This Book Will Get You Dreaming AND Achieving!

In these uncertain times, an action plan is more necessary than ever, and this book lays out the steps in practical, do-able ways. Entrepreneurs are going to save this country in this economic downturn; this book will help you to let go of your fears and start building on your own unique dreams to achieve them like never before.

—D. S. Beasley,
Owner, Angel Arts
(Colorado Springs)

Visualize Your Dreams To Live Your Dreams!

If you are looking to live your dreams or visualize your dreams—this book is for you. Living your dreams is not easy these days, especially in this down economy. Using a dream board or a vision board is often cited as one of the best ways to achieve your goals when striving for your dreams. I really enjoyed reading this book—highly insightful and very informative.

—Taylor Reaume, Search Engine Pros,
(Santa Barbara, CA)

THE NEWEST SECRET

Author Your Reality ACTION PLAN
Part 1: Introduction to Dream Planning

[Adapted and updated from The Original Dreams to Reality Series]

DEBORAH S. NELSON

Copyright © 2013 by Deborah S. Nelson.

ISBN: 978-0615834818

The author retains sole copyright to her contributions to this book.

Cover design by Omni Design.
budidana@yahoo.com

The interactive goal setting teaching model introduced in this series is patent pending; and may not be used without permission or a licensing agreement from DS Publishing Company.

Published by DS Publishing Company 3107 W Colorado Ave #303 Colorado Springs CO 80904

All Rights Reserved

No part of this book may be reproduced or used in any form without permission from the publisher. The original purchaser is hereby granted permission to print pages for personal use.

Copies of this may NOT be transmitted, stored, or recorded in any form without written permission from the publisher, DS Publishing Company, will prosecute any violations of copyright law, including e-mail attachments or any other means.

CONCEIVE

BELIEVE

RECEIVE

ACHIEVE

Acknowledgments

Gwen Ellis—*Seaside Creative Services*, Editor

Interior Book Design—Eugene Rijn Saratorio

Final Proofread: Liz Manduca, Manduca Music Publications

Jamie Nelson—*Jamie Nelson Studios,* Photographer

Alexa Davis—Believed in this work from the beginning

Renee Fontaine—Proficient Co-Dreamer

Audrey Addison Williams
—The 1st dreamer to prove this system works!

Dedication

To Mom

Who was my best friend.
In celebration of her joyful, cheerful, singing sayings.
Her light-hearted legacy lives on through my
daughter, who is now my best friend;

Mom would always say:
"Tomorrow is a new day
and the sun will come up tomorrow."

And she was right.

In life, we make certain decisions and implement choices.
Because of certain choices we may experience disappointment,
frustration, anger, fear, loneliness and sadness.
As emotional subside, buoyant energy returns and blossoms
Then, as if by magic, success and joy arise with the golden
morning sun
To lavish their liquid light all over those choices.
Thus, we begin to see our dreams come to reality.

Table of Contents

PART ONE: CONCEIVE

Chapter 1—Real Dreaming Takes Real Courage 29
Discover what you truly want and the reason we don't admit or state our desires. How and why we are trained to think small; identify your true **DREAM OBJECTIVE**.

Chapter 2—Trade Beliefs that Enslave for Beliefs that Serve 35
Identify personal, cultural, religious belief systems that guide thinking to limit outcomes because of the filtering system of beliefs that deny opportunities to grow.

Chapter 3—Acquire the Abundance Mindset 41
Thinking abundantly takes us out of limitation—the mindset that keeps us from enjoying abundance. Thinking abundantly is fertile ground for dreams to be born. Understanding comes for two major worldviews—competitive thinking versus creative thinking.

Chapter 4—Imagination: The Seed of Dreams 47
Breathe life into your dreams by stimulating, stretching, and motivating your imagination beyond its normal limits.

Chapter 5—The Power of the Pen 53
Those who write goals, visions, and dreams achieve them 20-to-one over those who don't. Write your dream script—the blueprint for a new life.

PART TWO: BELIEVE

Chapter 6—A Word about Words 61
It has been said that you are what you eat, but it can also be said that you are what you speak! Words frame our worldview.

Chapter 7—Reframe Failure to Deny Dream Deniers...................... 67
The concept of counter-intention. There will always be miserable people who wish to keep you in misery with them. Learn to think creatively to deny dream deniers.

Chapter 8—Building a Foundation of Faith..73
Be proactive. Dare to act out your dream before it arrives. Doubts are the projection of "not having your dream." Replace doubts with faith. Proactive faith gives the dream its motion.

Chapter 9—Energy, Entropy, and Momentum 79
David Hawkins' Chart of Consciousness, law of entropy, investing energy in your dreams, and stopping leakage of lower energy—emotions and false faith.

Chapter 10—Your Mind's Eye..85
Four different forms of expression and visualization. Jump start your enlightened visualization by shopping, test driving, taking photos, researching, field trips, and interviewing your heroes.

PART THREE: RECEIVE

Chapter 11—Activating the Thinking Stuff 93
Use a digital camera to take photos of your dream elements for your dream plan. Use *the workbook* in this series to write quotes, sayings, and significant thoughts.

Chapter 12—Ten Dream Steps for Success 99
Starting small, you develop your imagination muscle, your faith, and your vision. Once you start seeing the dream come to you, prepare to be a successful dream doer. Understanding past, present, and future. Your greatest power to act is in the present moment.

Chapter 13—Receive Your Dream 103
The difference between daydreaming and dream doing. One is fantasy; the other is fueled by inspired action. We block receiving

dreams because of our hesitation to believe it's real, and lack of thankfulness.

Chapter 14—The Practice of Gratitude 109
Staying connected with your source, or God, is key. Thankfulness is the most sincere and effective method for staying connected to the Creator who has made you to be creative.

Chapter 15—Be Careful What You Dream! 115
Live your dream and make the adjustments. Often when the dream shows up, the details are a little different than expected, and you may not recognize it. Constantly cultivate the awareness of, and the expectation that your dream is right here and right now.

FINAL: ACHIEVE

Chapter 16—Become a Dream Achiever 123
Create better dreams—dream of wonderful relationships, fulfilling career, amazing health and vitality—a beautiful environment, unique, exciting places to travel. Allow your dreams to impact those in your world in a positive way!

AUTHOR YOUR REALITY STEPS—
   Ten Author Your Reality Steps. 127

DICTIONARY OF TERMS—Key word definitions. 129

POWERFUL RESOURCES—Books, movies, and websites you may access to enhance and further your study and understanding of the *Author Your Reality Process.* 131

ABOUT THE AUTHOR—DEBORAH S. NELSON 135

CONCEIVE

BELIEVE

RECEIVE

ACHIEVE

Preface

THE SECRET BY Rhonda Byrne.
What an incredible breakthrough in human development! Second only to "What the Bleep Do We Know," for me, this work is among the most inspirational in the personal development genre of the first decade this century.

The Secret put the "Law of Attraction," on the radar screen of truth seekers, and dreamers and anyone who studies the science of success!

Yet . . . have you ever wondered why "the Secret" hasn't seemed to work for you? I HAVE!

The Human Potential Movement is a like a relay race. One development and breakthrough leads to another. And another. And another!

This book takes "The Law of Attraction" to the next level. Magically combined with the Power of the Pen and the principals of neurolinguistic psychology, we have a new breakthrough in attracting and bring our dreams into reality . . . on PURPOSE!

I have now proven this works with over 100 of my students who created a published physical manifestation of their dream, a vision book in self published form.

The Newest Secret is just that.

The Law of Attraction PLUS the Power of the Pen EQUALS Author Your Reality.

When you finish reading this book, purchase any one of the Author Your Reality workbooks, (Author Your Dreams, Author Your Career, Author Your Book, Author Your Relationship); and work through the 10 AUTHOR YOUR REALITY steps to create your own self-published Vision book; and Author Your New Reality, on purpose! Anyone can do this is 6 weeks!

If it is difficult for you go it on your own, go to the www.AuthorYourReality.com or www.newestsecret.com and find a course or online workshop to join with others who are supporting each other to complete their published vision books.

IT WILL CHANGE YOU LIFE . . . on purpose.

Deborah S. Nelson, Author,
The Newest Secret & *Author Your Reality Series*

Introduction to The Newest Secret

> "Man, alone, has the power to transform his thoughts into physical reality; man, alone, can dream and make his dreams come true."
>
> –Napoleon Hill

THIS BOOK SHARES some exciting news! We are created to dream and to see our dreams come true.

I enjoy the good fortune of living in a country during a time when women have the opportunity to grow into their own personhood. No longer are women in this country required to be dependents.

Perhaps I have experienced more than my share of dreams come true. Dare I dream yet another dream? Yes. It is to write, teach, and speak of the *author your reality* process. I dream this very moment that you will become an author yourself—the author of your dreams! Let me teach you how.

Some of us have had some dreams come true . . . sometimes. What if we could make our dreams come true on purpose and often?

This book breaks what I have labeled the *"author-your-reality process"* into four basic parts: conceive, believe, receive, and achieve. These are the key components of learning how to make your dreams come true—on purpose.

Some of the principles written in this book may appear to be spiritual or religious in nature. However, my approach to teaching the dreams to reality concept is practical. I leave spiritual and religious scholars to debate the rest. My mission is to transmit *author your reality* skills, not religion.

I quote from many sources including the Bible. And in full disclosure, I am a Christian, and I raised my daughter as such, sending her to Christian School. I do not attempt to associate my faith to the *"author your reality "*process. I share these principles as a practical matter.

The *author your reality* process is a skill set I have developed from 25 years of living, dreaming, reading, studying, self-development, failing, and succeeding. It is my understanding gleaned from hundreds of motivational books, books of wisdom, religious and spiritual learning. Seeing dreams come alive makes life full and rich!

I have attempted to present this information in a simple and organized manner, to allow for different learning styles, diverse spiritual backgrounds, as well as various educational and experience levels.

The *author your reality* process is a three-part series: this course book, a workbook, and a *published vision book,* which you will author. Yes, you will become the author of your own dreams—literally!

When you complete this series, you will receive your 7" x 7" 10 to 40-page *published vision book* via ground shipping.

Apply the ideas, concepts, and practices presented here and in the companion *workbook* to your daily life. Weave in your thoughts, wisdom, experience, knowledge, and faith in such a way that all your dreams may come true.

Happy dreaming!

Deborah S. Nelson

PART ONE
CONCEIVE

Chapter 1

Real Dreaming Takes Real Courage

"Toto, I don't think we're in Kansas, anymore."
–Dorothy, from The Wizard of Oz

Dream Come True or Fantasy?

LEE IACOCCA SAID, "The greatest discovery of my generation is that human beings can alter their lives by altering their attitudes of mind."

This book, with the corresponding workbook walks you through the formulation of your dream story, to the attraction, action, and arrival of your dream objective.

You will create a published dream script in the form of a 10 to 40-page book authored by you. That process alone will bring you to the brink of your dream. When you read, recite, and visualize your dreams using your personally published dream story, you will find it an invaluable tool and a powerful and effective attractor of your dreams.

Get ready to start some real dreaming. All you need to bring to this process is some real courage!

About Dreaming Big

Most of us have heard motivational speakers exhorting us to **DREAM BIG!** Although that may be realistic for them, most of us have weak "dreaming muscles." If we start by dreaming too big, we find we can't quite "lift the dream." We give up; thinking dreaming doesn't work at all! Weakly, we begin fantasizing instead of dream actualizing.

To DREAM BIG is an admirable and ultimate goal, and there's time for that. However, if we do not learn the baby dream steps carefully and consciously, we tend to dream too big, experience failure, and then, by default, fall back into the unfruitful habit of wishing-an incomplete form of dreaming.

What is a real dream—a true dream? The dreaming we teach starts with creating a vision, picture, word description, or a feeling of something desirable that you do not possess or experience at this moment. I call it the "dream object," or the "dream objective."

Starting with a small dream builds confidence through success. Once successful, you can then create and manifest bigger dreams using the same steps and process. As you build your dream manifestation ability, you will create bigger and better dreams, which will ultimately include dreams to make the world a better place for everyone—in your own personal way.

Getting Started by Tapping into Your Power

If we are in the habit of blaming circumstances and others for "our lot in life," we render ourselves powerless over our lives and circumstances. It takes courage to stop blaming and to take responsibility for the quality of our life and the way in which we see it. Once you stop blaming your parents, the past, the church, the government, the economy, your spouse, or your boss for shortcomings in your life, you will progress toward making your dreams come true. You will gain power to exhibit the courage to take the first step in the dreaming process!

This book does not promote religion, yet acknowledges one original Creator, who has created us in his image. This worldview understands that we are each creators of our circle of reality. We exercise the ability to create our environment, beliefs, obstacles, experiences, resulting overall mindset, and life experience.

In its purist form, this truth has us taking total responsibility for what our life is and what it will become. In order to be fluent in our ability to creatively visualize and manifest our dreams, we must take responsibility for what our lives look like right now. Then, and only then, we will wield the power to form the picture of the quality of life we so desire.

The Author Your Reality Process

The first thing to do to move our dreams to reality is to get started. Buying and reading this book and going through *the workbook* are beginning steps. Choosing a simple dream to turn into reality and to write about is the next step. Publishing your dream vision will follow. The final step is to receive your dream with open arms and complete gratefulness.

We have practiced the *author your reality* process all our lives with basic attributes such as walking and talking and eating and driving. These processes have become automatic. We take them for granted and we do not recognize them as earlier dreams come true.

At one time in our lives, basic activities we now take for granted such as singing, swimming, and driving were once dream objectives. We weren't able to do them. We had to first create a vision or a dream about being able to sing or swim or drive. We saw others doing these tasks and observed how convenient it was for them to have these skills. We formulated a picture of expectation, a group-dream objective that we would also accomplish these skills, and so within a few short months, we were singing, swimming, or driving as well.

Make "Failure" Your Mentor

What happened since those early days of fulfilling our primary dreams of singing, swimming, and driving? What stops us now from seeing our dreams fulfilled? Many factors have conspired against our successful dream doing.

First, the belief systems we have soaked up as children have taught us limitations—how to play it safe. Parents instilled those belief systems in us for our survival—for the most part.

Second, the concept of failure entered our lives. The idea of failure is like a candid snapshot taken at the worst possible moment. There actually is no such thing as so-called failure. Each so-called failure, when adjusted, guides us on through our course to success.

Third, most of us did not learn the dream actualizing process consciously. We do it subconsciously and randomly. Our subconscious dream realization is based on the limited belief systems we have acquired. We have conflicting "dream objectives" that may cancel each other out. Then we may find "negative dreams" coming true, and this further confirms our doubts about our ability to see happy dreams come true.

In order to see happy dreams come true, we need to identify our limiting belief systems and discover the fears that keep our real dreams hidden. Our "inherited fears" have intimidated us into replacing our real dreams with our parents' dreams or the culture's mediocre dreams. We trade our heartfelt inner passion for a mirage of external approval.

We need to realize that so-called failures are not giving-up points; rather they are steps to success. Facing the fear of failure and disappointment triggered when you start to identify what you truly want, takes a great deal of courage. *The workbook* in this series provides you with exercises (plays) to stimulate the discovery of what you really desire, and then to admit those dreams to yourself.

A Dream Come True—I Can't Believe It!

We are overjoyed when a long desired dream comes true! Often we say, "I can't believe it!" To believe it and receive it takes courage. Sometimes we send our dream away with a critical eye because it didn't show up quite as expected. Perhaps the dream is different than you thought it would be—the man of your dreams is a little bald or shorter than originally pictured. Your prince may be from another country, barely able to speak your language, and he's not 100 percent "dream prince." We think, *That is not what I had in mind!*

Yet at the same time, you observe that 95 percent of him may fit your dream prince. Do you ignore him and miss the opportunity to know him? Do you try to over-control the dream-situation and push him away? It's the unexpected differences that show up in the manifesting of our dreams that makes life so exciting and worth living!

If the love of your life entered your life like Cinderella's Prince Charming, would you be bored? After all, you know the end of that story. Cinderella didn't know the ending, and it was all very exciting for her! You may have noticed that her dream wasn't exactly picture perfect. She had jealous, ugly sisters and the meanest step-mom ever. And she was practically a slave for much of her childhood. Yet even in her misery, Cinderella learned to dream and she dreamed the love of her life right into her impossible situation!

When we set a course in motion for which we expect our dreams to come alive, we often find an unexpected twist or surprise when the dream arrives! Yet, once we receive the dream-gift with courage, confidence, and thankfulness, we discover it's our *imperfect dream formulation* that is blessing us as much as the dream itself. The dream is quite perfect, after all! So with courage in tow, let's go to the next chapter.

KEY POINTS TO REMEMBER

1. Summon up the courage for real dreaming.
2. Distinguish between fantasizing and actualizing.
3. Go inside to find a simple dream desire.
4. Find images and words to ignite your vision.
5. Formulate a draft dream vision on paper.

POWER STUDY FOR DREAMING WITH COURAGE

The Wizard of Oz, by Frank Baum (1939) is a film starring Judy Garland about a plain young girl from Kansas who finds herself in a mythical place and meets up with some other characters with big dreams. Together they go on a journey to make all their dreams come true!

Chapter 2

Trade Belief Systems that Enslave for Belief Systems that Free

"Ye shall know the truth and the truth shall set you free!"
—Jesus Christ

Belief Systems that Enslave

THE REASON I asked you to bring your courage with you to this chapter is that you are truly going to need it! *The workbook* will challenge you to dig deeply into your belief systems—those that you have subconsciously adopted as "unquestioned assumptions."

These unquestioned assumptions have been so deeply implanted into our psyche that we barely sense them there. They are deeply held and deeply hidden assumptions such as: "I'll never look good enough," and, "No matter how hard I work, I will always be in poverty," and, "No matter how hard I try, I'm not good enough."

As human beings, we have "caught" these assumptions from parents, teachers, religion, and culture and have rarely questioned them. They have become as invisible as the air; but nonetheless, they are powerful limiting influences.

If we were to strip away these beliefs, we would feel as if we were literally floating in space without gravity. Belief systems give us structure and purpose by creating a sort of psychic gravity so that we can move through the space of our life with direction.

People without strong belief structures may find themselves living lives many of us would consider unfulfilled, unethical, unlawful, and unsuccessful. We consider these lives as not contributing to society or as subtracting from everyone who comes in contact with them. We hold on tightly to our limiting belief structures, lest we become like them.

False or limiting belief systems are those that keep us in bondage to something that does not serve our best interests. Belief systems have their purpose, but at some point those of us who want to become successful dream doers drop old belief systems that no longer serve our highest aspirations.

Belief Systems Are Powerful

Beliefs are incredibly powerful. Whatever you believe as true actually becomes true for you and your circle of influence. "The Self-Imprisoned Bird" by Tom Russell is an incredible story that demonstrates the power of our beliefs.

The Self-Imprisoned Bird

Several years ago my wife and I were in Colorado for a speaking engagement. We had an afternoon free and visited the local zoo, sauntering back to the exotic bird section. We saw a circular fence, probably 18 feet high and some 60 feet across. It was very odd to us that the fence had no top to it.

We observed a rare bird in a far corner. I reasoned that the keepers must have clipped its wings so it could not fly away. Then, suddenly, the bird went into full flight to a tree on the other side of the cage. Obviously, I was wrong. The bird's wings were fine. I found a zoo attendant and asked why the bird didn't fly away. "The reason is very simple," he said. "This bird was raised in captivity. When it was young, it was placed in a cage with a top on it. Every time it tried to fly away, it would hit the ceiling. Now the bird never tries to escape. It is convinced the top of the cage is still there.

This story is a demonstration of how we can let belief systems limit us in our ability to soar to the heights of our dreams.

Belief Systems that Set You Free

"Ye shall know the truth and the truth shall set you free," said Jesus Christ. It is one of the most important truths in the Bible. When Jesus spoke of truth, it wasn't about "the rules" or religious practices. He broke "the rules." Against the prevailing belief systems of the day, he healed on the Sabbath Day. He said things such as, "Let the dead bury their dead," and "The poor will always be with you." His point was that there is a bigger truth than "the rules," and if we desire freedom, we will discover and honor the truth for ourselves. We cannot be bound to "the rules," if we seek truth.

The Power of the Present Moment

The simplest way to live the truth is to live in the present moment where the greatest power is. If we are connected with our Creator in the present moment, we will automatically know our true desires, true strengths, and true talents. God gives us the "desires of our heart," another powerful truth from the Bible. It is God who plants those unique desires into our hearts.

Therefore, our heart's wisdom is something to be trusted. To follow our desires requires courage since we are required to explore our hearts and to act on intuition and faith, rather than taking the advice of authority. In doing so, we risk the ridicule of those who make and keep the rules. However, those in authority often do not have our best interests at heart. They may not even be aware of the agenda they serve. Many in authority, such as doctors, executives, and politicians, are selling something: pharmaceuticals, fast food, fashion, and policy. There is nothing wrong with these things, but it is important that we know who we are, and what we need in the present moment. It is the only way to avoid becoming a slave to another's greed, selfishness, or bottom line.

As we become trained consumers and trained workers, our imagination is recruited to other agendas, which slowly robs us of desire, passion, and creativity. We are no longer whole people while we serve someone else's vision, lifestyle, and pocketbook.

Investing in Ourselves Wisely

Living in the present moment takes courage, honesty, and self-understanding. Investing in yourself creates the biggest payoff ever! We simply need to take time to be aware and honest with ourselves regarding the reruns we play in our minds and hearts over and over again.

Often, those reruns are about an emotional trauma that we have not resolved. Training ourselves to live in the present moment gives us answers. We must confront the "pain-body," spoken of by Eckhart Tolle, to reside in the present moment, and to experience true healing and wholeness.

Awareness of those situations in which we invest our energy, money, and time that do not serve and enhance our true self is key. Aware of who we are in the present moment, we realize we have been doing almost everything for approval. "Some would sell their own soul to gain the whole world," is another truth spoken by Jesus. He is saying that when we sell our souls, what we get is temporary external approval. That is not investing in ourselves. It's investing in those who are robbing us of integrity, autonomy, independence—and our soul.

To Know Thyself, Is to Love Thyself

As we begin to invest in ourselves and begin to know our true selves, we gain freedom from our imprisoning belief systems, whether they are mediocre cultural beliefs, parents' misappropriated expectations, or guilt-producing religious dogmas. Once you reach adulthood and become an independent person, you no longer need the approval of those around as you once did in order to survive the precarious early years of life.

Once you free yourself from false and limiting beliefs, true approval comes from within. Each day you can honestly say to yourself, "I accept, love, and approve of myself just as I am and

I am thankful for this." This powerful inner truth practiced in the present moment is the beginning of creating a powerful belief system to free you to be your most incredible, beautiful, powerful, loving self! *Ye shall know the truth and the truth shall set you free'*. Now why not pick up your newly-found freedom from false beliefs and come on over to Chapter 3.

KEY POINTS TO REMEMBER

1. Subconscious belief systems can be enslaving.
2. Awareness heals false-belief agendas.
3. Investing in yourself is the best investment.
4. To know yourself is to love yourself.
5. Adopt a truthful belief system that sets you free.

POWER STUDY FOR THE SUBJECT OF BELIEF

What the Bleep Do We Know? Documentary by Captured Light Industries and A Lord of the Wind film. This movie is a documentary of interviews with scientists and spiritualists involved in research of quantum physics and where reality meets physics. The focus is how the observer alters the physics of reality by his beliefs and expectations.

Website: www.whatthebleep.com.

[1.] Paul Bauer, *Dreams Alive: Secrets of Manifesting Action Series*, 2007.
[2.] Tom Russell, *Super Wisdom, Seven Powerful Secrets for a Rich and Purpose-Filled Life*, 2006.
[3.] Eckhart Tolle, *The Power of Now;* 1999, Namaste Publishing.

Chapter 3

Acquire the Abundance Mindset

> "Abundance is not something we acquire. It is something we tune into."
>
> –Dr. Wayne Dyer

Desiring Abundance

NOW THAT YOU are in the process of freeing yourself from false, negative, and enslaving beliefs, the next step in bringing your dream closer to you is to replace limiting beliefs with an amazing, truthful, productive, unlimited, and abundant belief system.

Be patient with yourself, as this is not an overnight event. Cultivating awareness of enslaving beliefs and replacing them with new beliefs is groundbreaking work. Strategically done, your new beliefs will provide the psychic structure for you to become the best version of yourself, and position you to actualize all your dreams. Tuning into an abundance mindset is the beginning of finding a new empowering belief system.

Before we go into how to develop an abundance mindset, let us have a little chat about two worldviews—the competitive worldview and the creative worldview. These are represented by positive thinking and truthful thinking.

Positive Thinking

Positive thinking is a good thing, right? Well, maybe yes, maybe no. I have always sensed there was something not quite right about the concept of positive thinking. On the surface, it sounds good. But after reading books, attending workshops, and listening to "celebrity speaker experts" on the subject, I have reached the conclusion that "positive thinking" is good, but not good enough for those of us on a quest to "go the distance" in seeking our dreams.

Truthful Thinking

One day I was listening to audiotapes by Anthony Robbins and was overjoyed to find him addressing the subject I have personally dubbed the *Holy Grail of Positive Thinking*. He mentioned, quite humorously, that to go out to the garden and speak, "There are no weeds, there are no weeds, there are no weeds," is not the best technique for getting rid of weeds!

I laughed out loud upon hearing the illustration. In absorbing that powerful picture, an awareness of the truth swept over me and freed me from belief that it was my "stinking thinking" keeping me from the success I knew was mine. I had just dissolved another limiting belief! *The truth is more powerful than positive thinking.* Deep down inside, I knew success was mine, but mental gymnastics wasn't going bring it to me.

Positive thinking is an external process. You tell yourself to alter your thoughts to think differently after you already thought the thoughts. That's not the truth. The truth is inside you. The truth is more powerful than positive thinking, because positive thinking is just another pretty lie.

Competitive Worldview or Creative Worldview

This brings us to the worldview to which your mind naturally gravitates:

- In the world there is not enough of anything (competitive worldview)
- The world is a place of unlimited abundance (creative worldview)
- The world is a safe place, a friend place (creative worldview)
- The world is a place where survival is king (competitive worldview)

Consider with which overall worldview that your mind feels most comfortable and the state of your mind resides in most represented by the statements above.

Crabs in the Bucket

To demonstrate the competitive viewpoint, I am reminded of crabs in a bucket. Their eminent destiny is to be either someone's dinner, or to escape the bucket.

The bucket doesn't need a lid to keep the crabs contained because if there is more than one crab, none of the crabs will let the others escape to freedom. If one tries to get out, they pull it back into the bucket. This is what human beings do to each other in a competitive environment. If someone is about to succeed, the group pulls him or her down to a level of mediocrity, misery, or even death.

Those of us determined to reach the peak of our destiny have extra work ahead to escape the crabs of society. At times, understandably, we are tempted to give in to a life of comfort and mediocrity. The problem with this "easy life" is that death is just one meal away! A little too much TV, a little too much fast food, and high blood pressure caused by the stress of living, working, and contending with crabs could turn into a heart attack and death at any moment.

Creative Thinking

Remember the story of the bird in the zoo? At one point there was a top on its cage, but once the top was removed, the bird continued to fly against the sides and did not try to escape through the top. That bird and the crabs have much in common. They believe they are stuck right where they are. Yet the crabs could band together to form a chain to escape the bucket, the bird could fly vertically instead of horizontally to fly up and out to freedom.

In order to escape the base survival level, creative and truthful thinking must be cultivated. If we continue to think and act competitively and horizontally, we remain stuck at a level where the masses of mediocrity and misery exist, unable to escape to freedom. If we continue doing the same actions expecting different results, we become unhealthy. As we raise our thinking to a higher level, we will joyously fly to new heights with the wings of freedom God has given us.

Powerful Thinking Stuff

How do we think creatively, truthfully, and abundantly? We start by practicing seeing the world as a place of abundance and realizing that there is plenty for all and that there is a "thinking stuff from which all things are made." Wallace D. Wattles in 1910 writes the following:

"There is a thinking stuff from which all things are made, and which, in its original state, permeates, penetrates, and fills the interspaces of the universe. A thought in this substance produces the thing that is imaged by the thought."

There have been many books written on the subject of abundance and riches, but the book entitled, *The Science of Getting Rich,* is the most revolutionary and effective book on the study of abundance I have ever read.

When you thoroughly grasp that all wealth and abundance, including that of mind, soul, and body, comes from the "thinking stuff and that the "thinking stuff is totally unlimited, your mind shifts from a competitive station to the creative network.

The Creative Mindset

The creative mindset is connected to God—the source—and the universe. There are many ways to tap into your source. While some find it through meditation and prayer, others find it through nature. Still others connect to their source by practicing thankfulness. The important thing is to connect directly and daily to your source. It is not necessary to go through an authority, a guru, a religious figure, or even by using a certain method or technique. In fact, using a third party to connect with your Creator is ineffective.

Find your own way and specific times for connecting with Source. You will find truth, creativity, and yourself. Rather than thinking horizontally, you will begin to think vertically! You will not be stuck in the bucket with crabs, hopelessly and desperately trying to climb out. Instead your will position yourself to receive creative solutions coming from your Creator, and by being in that quiet and powerful space, you can begin to define and make your dreams come true.

KEY POINTS TO REMEMBER

1. Becoming aware of your limiting beliefs is a process.
2. Replace limiting beliefs with empowering beliefs.
3. Tune into the mindset of abundance.
4. Learn to think vertically and creatively.
5. Plant your dream-ideas into "the thinking stuff."

POWER STUDY FOR ACQUIRING AN ABUNDANCE MINDSET

The Science of Getting Rich, by Wallace D. Wattles, originally published 1910.

This book was written in the early 1900s and addresses the importance of developing an abundant mindset. He advocates that it is crucial for people to live lives rich in all ways—physical, mental, spiritual—and that to do so requires a certain mindset.

Free PDF of the book, www.scienceofgettingrich.net

Chapter 4

Imagination — Seed of Dreams

"The power of Thought, the magic of the Mind!"
–Lord Byron

Imagination

AS I WRITE this chapter, coincidentally, today is John Lennon's birthday. Whether we agree with his politics or not, he was a great creator, dreamer, and visionary. His song, *Imagine*, voices profound dream-action for the entire world. In this song written by Lennon, he admits being a dreamer and invites listeners to join him in a magnificent dream for all of mankind.

Imagination Extinction

The concept of the "thinking stuff introduced in the last chapter, presents the unlimited field where we will paint our imaginative visions. First, however, we will need to revive our imaginations once again.

With television, movies, and the Internet, our mind-space is bombarded with endless images and messages. The challenge for dream doers with this information overload is to take control of mind-space. How glorious it is to begin to plant our own images, words, thoughts, ideas, and messages into the universal mind-space.

Let's become aware of information, images, and ideas we allow to enter our mind-space. If our mind is over crowded with corporate agendas spoon-fed to us through advertising, we can be distracted from serving our own vision. In fact, it is common for our ideas, thoughts, and inspirations to become casualties to the idea that we are required to "make a living."

Making a Living

This is a primary concern. Nearly our entire lives are caught up in the unquestioned assumption that we need "to make a living." We have been taught, trained, and indoctrinated all our lives that we must "make a living!"

As we grow to adulthood, we receive instruction and training from every angle and by all medias on how to make an even better living—a better living being defined with newer cars, larger homes, designer clothes, stuff, and then newer stuff. There is nothing wrong with stuff. Yet, as we become slaves to stuff, we give up major real estate of our mind-space to the ever-growing task of making an even better living. *We work to live and live to work!* There is little or no space left over to cultivate our imagination in order to build our dreams and see them fulfilled.

I believe the idea that we must have a constantly escalating lifestyle is one of the biggest lies ever perpetuated. Think about it. You are alive. I am alive. We were created to live. Therefore, why should we lean over the Creator's shoulder to instruct him how to keep us alive? This whole "making a living" doctrine has been shoved into our minds and hearts our whole lives, and I, for one, proclaim that it's not true.

How Do I Feed My Family and Myself?

How do I feed myself then? How do I make money, you ask? I can't feed my children on imagination. Those, dear reader, are horizontal questions, and in order to deal with them, we'll have to fly out of top of the cage and think creatively. *Go to the source to get your source.* Our imagination needs to come alive. We need to discover its ability to breathe life into our dreams. When our imagination is tied up with the business of "making a living" and in living the lifestyle of corporate crabs, our imagination dies.

The Best Investment You Will Ever Make

The best investment you will ever make is in yourself. It's true, that when you invest in yourself directly, you will not get a weekly or monthly paycheck right away. It may take months and years before you ever see any real self-employment income. Yet investing in books, workshops, seminars, and self-development tools is an investment in uncovering the layers of limited beliefs; and agendas that we serve in exchange for so-called financial security, approval, status, and elitism.

Once you withdraw your need for approval, you will gain the necessary energy and time to invest in yourself, which is the best investment ever. There are ways to change the channel and free up your mind's imagination to work in your favor. You no longer need fatten another's pocketbook—as a consumer or as a worker. Here's a short list of ways to free up mental real estate:

1. Minimize your television consumption.
2. Cut consumables-eating out, pay TV, big holiday gifts.
3. Invest in yourself with classes, books, seminars, etc.
4. Observe whether you are consuming or producing.

Celebration of Imagination

As we free up mental real estate, we naturally start to use our imagination to discover our dream objectives. Depending on our ability to imagine, at first we may come up with dreams such as, "I want $250,000 a year," or "I dream that I am driving a Harley Davidson motorcycle." There is no dream too big or too small. Tap into your wants and desires, and ask yourself, "Once I get the $250,000 a year, what will it do for me? Once I get that Harley, what is it about that big hog that gives me pleasure or joy?" Once you get the money, what will you spend it on? The answers reveal your deeper dreams.

The answer may be that you will be able to spend more time with family. That's okay if that's your dream objective, since in that case, it's not really the money you want, but a way to nurture a relationship. As for the Harley, perhaps the dream objective is to feel the wind in your hair and have the freedom to get away from it all. So ask yourself, "What is the idea behind the initial dream idea?" Get down to the real dream objective.

Dream Objective

We will start with one dream objective to write about and publish. Based on your dream objective you create, a 10 to 40-page published vision book to read, review, and to release the "thinking stuff." This process awakens and stimulates your imagination to breathe life into your dream.

We are going to start with four areas from which you can choose your dream objective. These areas come from the acronym S-E-L-F.

S stands for space. That covers your home, office, car, and how you move about. It includes how you move, function, and travel within your space. Perhaps you have a dream to go to Europe for the first time in your life. Or perhaps you would like to remodel a room in your home for improved use of space. Write down your dream for your space.

E is for energy. What kind of dream objectives might you formulate in the area of energy? Energy refers to your physical health, spiritual, and professional development, and anything else that would provide energy to your life. Perhaps you have an objective to give up drinking sodas or you want to get into an effective exercise program. Write down your energy objectives.

L refers to your love relationships, your family, spouse, friends. Do you have a dream in the area of relationships? Perhaps you want to attract the love of your life, or you want to see romance return to your main love-relationship. Write it in your workbook.

F stands for financial. A dream object might be to create $500 for the objective of reducing credit card debt, thereby earning a measure of freedom from consumerism. A financial dream objective might be to attract an extra $200 a month to pay for classes for a real estate license. Identify and write down a financial dream.

Choose Your Dream Objective

For your first dream story, I suggest keeping it simple. You want to be successful right in the beginning so you can build up your dream muscles. Choose something that you can be excited about, and as time goes on, something about which you can be passionate.

KEY POINTS TO REMEMBER

1. Take your mind-space back.
2. Imagination gives the breath of life to your dreams.
3. Begin to allow your imagination to stretch and grow.
4. Select an area to define a dream objective.
5. Select a dream objective, something that excites you.

POWER STUDY FOR "MAKING A LIVING"

Do What You Love, The Money will Follow, Marsha Sinetar, 1989 Random House.

Website: www.marshasinetar.com.

This book advocates the importance of finding your gifts, and strengths and making *them* your highest priority, rather than making money your highest priority. Sinetar's bold premise is that once you are ignited with the joy of doing what you love, the money will follow.

Chapter 5

The Power of the Pen

"Go confidently in the direction of your dreams! Live the life you've imagined."

–Henry David Thoreau

The Invention of the Printing Press

THE INVENTION OF the printing press was one of the most transformational inventions in modern history. Once the printing press was invented, knowledge became accessible to the common man, and mass education was possible.

Publishing houses, Bibles, and encyclopedias became plentiful, but it was very expensive to publish a book. The set-up process was time consuming, making it necessary to publish in quantities of thousands upon thousands to make even one book affordable.

With the development of digital printing, it is now possible to print just one book in full color and with amazing quality. *Author Your Reality* is going to teach you how to write and print your own book. Now anyone who knows how to read, write, and has a PC and the Internet can be their own publisher. With this process, you become a published author, author of your dreams.

Author of Your Dreams

About three to five percent of the population actually takes the time to write down their goals and dreams. Maybe that is why so few people actually live the life they dream about. Writing is the magical point where your ideas, passions, and desires begin to materialize. We are going to take our desires and passions and synthesize them into a series of positive statements. These statements will create a story, and this will be the first symbolic representation of dreams put into words on paper. Stephen Covey said, "All things are created twice. There's a mental or first creation, and a physical or second creation of all things. You begin with the end in mind."

The reason the pen is powerful and the written word is so magical is because the written word is like a bridge from imagination to reality—a physical point where imagination enters the physical realm. With the power of the pen, you can write out the endpoint of your dreams!

Creating Your Story

The workbook will walk you through specific steps, and for this part of the process, you will need pencil and paper; or just write in your workbook for this action plan. Begin by choosing an area where you want to bring a dream into reality. Choose from one of the following areas:

Relationships
Career and Finance
Health and Well Being
Home, Office, and Travel Environment
Spiritual, Personal, and Professional Development

Once you have selected an area from which to create your dream, write it down.

Procrastination

Did you get a piece of paper and write down the area in which you want to create your *published vision book?* The reason I ask, after just telling you to do it, is because so many of us are prone to procrastination. Procrastination is the fear of doing something—the fear that we may not be able to do it, so we put it off "till later." But, somehow, "later" never comes. Fear creates its own reality.

I encourage you to take advantage of this amazing opportunity to learn how to live your dreams right now. The most powerful moment in your life is right now. If you make a mistake, you can correct it right now. However, it is not a mistake to act right now on opportunities that you have attracted to yourself! So, if you haven't grabbed a pencil, paper, or the workbook, please do so "right now." I want you to succeed in all your dreams. Choose a category from the list above about which you want to make a dream.

Why Wait? Imagine it Now!

Pick one dream from one category—one that stirs up deep desire and drive within you! Close your eyes and imagine the best possible scenario of the dream you want to become real. Compose a sentence to describe your dream and write it down. If you have always wanted to travel to Italy, make the statement, "I travel to Italy for an entire month next year." Locate magazine or travel brochure photos of Italy. Scan them into your computer to form the basics of your dream script.

Fill in the Dream Script

Take the next few days and weeks to identify feelings and reasons why you love Italy and why you want to go there. Let your mind and imagination wander. If there is a friend or family member you hope to visit there, get in touch with them and ask for a photo of them and their home and other photos of the area where they live.

Consider taking Italian lessons at the local adult education center. Buy CDs of how to speak Italian and begin to practice. Scan bits and pieces from the Italian classes or Italian curriculum into your computer to incorporate into your dream script that will take you to Italy.

Look for pictures of Italian poetry, food, songs, clothing, shoes, landmarks, and any other things you want to see and do while in Italy. You can feel that the one sentence, "I am traveling to Italy for a month by the end of next year," sets your imagination and creativity in motion.

Once you start uploading images to the book publishing software, you will be amazed how wonderful it looks. These images will be incorporated into your dream script, which will become a real book! Select a beautiful photo for the front and back cover. You will also want to write some introductory copy for the back cover!

Write and Publish Your Dreams

The *Author Your Reality Vision Book* offers 10 to 40-pages to record your dream story. Rely heavily on photos and artwork that moves you. One year in my dream script, I stated that I wanted to travel globally. I wasn't specific as to where. To enhance the wording, I used clip art of buildings that looked exciting to me. I chose the Eiffel Tower in Paris. Additionally, I also chose a photo of some random ruins I thought looked magnificent.

The next spring, my daughter's photos were selected for an art show in Rome. When she told me about it, I immediately said, "Let's go." I have always wanted to go to Europe." (What better excuse needed, right?) My daughter purchased airline tickets, and I used my vacation rental property here in the United States [another story in itself] to trade for our lovely accommodations in Europe. Once our dream is presented to the universe, money isn't the issue we often think it will be.

Paris and Rome Pictured

It was incredible . . . the girls (my daughter and her best friend) booked airline tickets first to Paris for a week, and then to Rome for the art show. Of course, we visited the Eiffel Tower, which was one of the pictures in my dream script. Now we have fabulous photos of the three of us standing in front of the Eiffel Tower!

When we arrived in Rome for the art show, to my utter amazement, I saw it! I saw the ruins from the clip art in my dream script! They were from Rome! It was breathtaking and I was overwhelmed when I recognized the ruins. It is nothing short of miraculous how the subconscious attracts situations and events related to our vision. Once you decide, write, and publish your dream script, you can expect that soon you, too, will be running with your dreams.

The Power of Attraction and Action

Once you have written your dream script, a story begins to form; and reading it, imagining it, feeling it, and reciting it to yourself will inspire the universe to attract people and events into your sphere of influence. With your vision constantly present in your mind's eye, your desire to take action is increased.

Instead of trying to motivate yourself with discipline, rules, and belief systems, you will be inspired to action. You will be pulled by the vision in your dreams, and find the actions necessary to bring your dreams into the reality, with little or no difficulty. Dreams pull and beliefs push. Free yourself from beliefs and their accompanying rigors of discipline and replace them with a life of dreams manifested *by inspired action.*

KEY POINTS TO REMEMBER

1. Choose an area for fulfilling a dream now.
2. Write on paper to bring your vision into "your now."
3. Stating your dreams on paper inspires ownership.

4. Find exciting images to create your published vision book.
5. Write your dream statement—review it, read it, imagine it.

POWER STUDY FOR THE POWER OF NOW

The Power of Now, By Eckhart Tolle; 1999, Namaste Publishing. This book teaches the incredible power of the present moment, and gives ways to overcome living in the past and projecting fears into the future.

Website: www.eckharttolle.com

PART TWO
BELIEVE

Chapter 6

A Word About Words

> "Thoughtless words create thoughtless realities. Design your thoughts and speak your words to create your own best reality."
>
> –Deborah S. Nelson

The World of Words

WHERE WOULD YOUR mind go if I said, "Don't think of a pink elephant!" Your mind jumps to a pink elephant, doesn't it? Your mind does not hear the "DON'T," it recognizes the "pink elephant" part of the sentence. We are constantly speaking to our subconscious mind, but it does not function in the literal; rather, it is like a child who only hears the pictures you speak to it.

This is where the application of the concept of positive thinking can be effective. When we make statements without using negatives, our speaking becomes exponentially more effective. Negatives include such words as "no," "don't," "won't," "can't," "shouldn't," etc. We train ourselves to avoid these words, because the mind will go right to where you tell it NOT to go, and that's because it only hears the visual part of the sentence.

The subconscious mind understands the language of pictures more than it does words. You write the script to the powerful subconscious mind with your word pictures; and the mind creates the pictures that you send it.

What You Focus on Is What You Get

Your mind is such a powerful attractor and creative force that it will conspire to manifest what you focus on. If you focus on what you DON'T WANT, that's what you will attract. It's important to change the focus and create word pictures of what you DO WANT. Use powerful words when speaking to yourself. Change your self-talk from "have to" and "should," to "I want to," "I choose to," and "I will." Completely remove the words "can't," "no way," "impossible," and the "what ifs," from your vocabulary.

You Are What You Speak

We have all heard the expression, "You are what you eat," and that may be true, but I would like to add that *you are what you speak!*

Words are powerful, but how powerful are they? Are they powerful because they represent your thoughts, or do they actually create your thoughts? Take charge of your life and design your thoughts to create words that will in turn create your reality. Don't allow thoughtless words to create a thoughtless reality. Your true thoughts come from inside and your best thoughts come from your source. Discover them and express them as your own unique understanding of the world.

It has been studied, proven, and is generally accepted that attitude creates your reality. We know that on the day we have a great attitude life seems to treat us better, and on days we have a bad attitude life seems to treat us badly.

Your Words Are the Boss

What we speak is "under heard" by our subconscious, and it reacts. If we ask our subconscious, "What is wrong with me?" it will seek an answer. Accordingly, if we ask "What is right with me?"

it will seek an answer. The questions we mumble to ourselves, and the statements we say out loud, create a "word image," a self-image of how we see ourselves, and how we relate to the world.

Self Talk Equals Self Image

Our self-image is created by the words we speak. Truly, whatever we say to ourselves (and others), our mind believes and tries to rationalize to be in harmony with those self-beliefs. Anorexic people continue to starve themselves because they keep telling themselves they are fat. They see their "fat image" in the mirror because that's what their word pictures tell them. Our words are powerful. You could say our words are the creators of thoughts, attitudes, and ultimately, our reality.

That is why people trying to stop smoking have difficulty. They tell themselves "I can't smoke cigarettes anymore." But their subconscious mind interprets the "smoke cigarettes" as the dominant word picture and it continues to be drawn to smoking cigarettes. The effective way to quit a bad habit is to substitute the habit with something else. That way you aren't focusing on what you don't or can't want, but on what you do want.

Focus on What You Want with Words

If you want your dreams to come true, it is best to focus on the dream itself, not on what you don't want! If you focus on what you don't want, that's what you get. The definition of insanity is doing and saying the same thing over and over again and expecting different results!

Give Yourself Power with Your Words

When you blame circumstances and other people for what you don't like in your life, you are giving your power away. Remember, *the present doesn't equal the past.* At any given moment you can change your patterns, thoughts, words, and your life! Take your power back by using empowering words. Instead of saying, "I can't do this anymore," try the more powerful words, "*I choose to do something better for myself.*" "I want to do that which makes me a better person." Instead of "*I have to,*" replace the sentence with "*I choose to,*" or " *I want to,*" or "*I am going to.*" Now you take control of your life. As your subconscious mind takes orders from your words and thoughts, you move forward to a better place by using more powerful words!

Speak in the Present Tense

Give your words even more power by speaking about your dreams in the present tense. You have no power to change the past and you can't act in the future. Therefore, the powerful present moment is yours to wield! When you state your desire to dream, state and imagine it as if it has already come true. By creating a *published vision book,* you will review, recite, and visualize your dream on a daily basis. This will give form to the vision you have planted in the "thinking stuff." This dream vision planted, attracts circumstances for you to act with inspired action, and to believe, receive, and achieve your dream.

Positive Words and Positive Thinking

Remember in an earlier chapter I sited Tony Robbins' example of speaking to the weeds, "There are no weeds, there are no weeds, there are no weeds, there are no weeds . . ." with the expectation for the weeds to magically disappear. This is an example of trying to make positive thinking and positive speaking do magic. But what is the truth of the situation?

1. The weeds exist, as the object of denial.
2. The weeds are not wanted.
3. Perhaps it's best to just pull up the weeds.

Truthful Thinking

Truthful thinking might interject, "What are these weeds anyway? Are they some kind of herb that might be helpful? Could they be cultivated and harvested?"

Dandelions, treated as weeds in lawns, are also harvested and sold as herbs. Truthful thinking would likely say, "Accept that the weeds are weeds. Love the weeds; they arrived on the scene for a purpose. Thank the weeds! Truly be thankful that you have the land that even has the weeds." Allow the intuitive mind to discover the purpose of the weeds in your life.

KEY POINTS TO REMEMBER

1. Thoughts become things.
2. The truth trumps positive thinking.
3. You are what you speak.
4. Find out the truth daily and speak the truth.
5. Discipline words and thinking to reflect inner truth.

POWER STUDY FOR THE POWER OF WORDS

Psycho-Pictography: The New Way to Use the Miracle Power of Your Mind, By Vernon Howard, 1965 by Parker Publishing Company, Inc. Vernon Howard used the power of word stories and parable visualization to teach the ages' greatest wisdom.

Chapter 7

Reframe Failure to Deny Dream Deniers

"I merely took the energy it takes to pout and wrote some blues."

–Duke Ellington

When it All Seems to Go Wrong

DREAM DENIERS COME in many forms. Be aware of:

Guilt
Jealous
Envy
Misery
Fear
Loneliness
Frustration
Anger
Manipulation

Strangers, friends, family, co-workers, your spouse, and even including yourself, will try to pull out all the stops to keep you from progressing in your dreams. Take Note: Forgive them—they do not realize they are doing this, nor do you realize you are doing this to yourself, either!

Why? They, and we, prefer to stay right in the middle of the comfort zone. As you move into your dreams, they will see you joyful, abundant, growing, and happy. The contrast of your joy and their misery may cause them discomfort.

Past Patterns and Dynamics

When you start moving into new success, at first you are not used to it. You find yourself on one hand ecstatic; but on the other hand, you are waiting for the other shoe to drop. Even your biochemistry is expecting something to happen to take it all away from you. Your nervous system is not used to the abundant, peaceful, successful life. Let's bring a little drama in to spice things up! Let's get the adrenalin running. Let's make life difficult. It can't be this easy! When you see this scenario developing and become aware of it, expose the pattern by reminding yourself, *"The past does not equal the future!"*

Counter Intention

This is a concept I learned from Paul Bauer's teachings on the subject of manifesting. By understanding this powerful concept we can more easily see our dreams come true. Often we interrupt the manifestation of our dreams with counter intention.

Counter intention is the idea that once we set our intent in a direction, we begin to obsessively look for our dream to appear in reality. This is akin to the old expression, "A watched pot never boils." If we do not see change right away or within the time frame expected, we may jump to the conclusion that, "It's not going to happen," or "It's not working."

It is important to be aware of counter intention because a major premise in seeing our dreams come true is to visualize the desired outcome and focus on that outcome with pictures, affirmations, thoughts, and feelings. However, if you begin "counter intending" you can stop the forward progress of your dream by focusing on the thought that, "It's not happening." This is because we get what we focus on, and if we are focusing on how it's not coming true, or how we don't have enough, then we interrupt the forward progress of the dream. As we catch ourselves counter intending, we may gently guide our thoughts and feelings back to the desired outcome.

Doubt, Fear, Worry

The best thing to do when we see doubt, fear, and worry undermining our progress is to become aware of these emotions. Become a negative emotion detector. Once you detect negative emotions, realize they are symptoms that can be helpful to you. Facing fear, doubt, and worry can be stressful, but burying them is even more stressful. The sooner these negative emotions are uncovered, and you get to the source of them, the sooner you will undergo transformational realizations.

Helpful techniques to confront fear, worry, and doubt include meditation, affirmations, prayer, and breathing. Be still and face distracting fears, worries, and doubts keeping you from focusing on the big picture of your positive, happy, joyful vision!

A lot of what this involves is the process of "letting go," which can be a challenge if you do not realize that's what needs to be done. Once you gain access to an underlying negative core belief, it is a simple matter to realize that it is not the truth. It is something you have adopted as a defense mechanism. Once you shine the light of your awareness on these negative emotions, and see them as "smoke and mirrors" hiding deep and underlying negative core beliefs, it's a matter of moments before those negative belief structures dissolve.

When the Dream Seems Not to Go Right

One thing that can work to turn these upsets around is to realize that even though it does not seem to be going right, suspend judgment for just a minute. PRETEND it is going right. Pretend there is a reason that the thing going wrong has an unseen purpose.

This pretense is to change your perspective, and it is not meant to be a denial of truth.

Once you set a dream intent in motion, the universe conspires to make it happen; and there is sometimes a strange roundabout way that things are brought about. Understand that any "upset" is a small puzzle—piece to the entire larger picture. Stay in faith and you will find that the so-called "failure" was really a great success.

A student had set his mind on making a certain business combination, which seemed to him at the time to be very desirable, and he worked for some weeks to bring it about. When the crucial time came, the thing failed in a perfectly inexplicable way. It was as if some unseen influence had been working secretly against him. But he was not disappointed. On the contrary, he thanked God that his desire had been overruled and went steadily on with a grateful mind.

In a few weeks, an opportunity so much better came his way that he would not have made had the first deal worked out. He saw a mind, which knew more than he knew, had prevented him from losing the greater good. It kept him from entangling himself with the lesser of two opportunities.

That is the way every seeming failure will work out for you if you keep your faith, hold to your purpose, have gratitude, and do every day all that can be done that day, and do each separate act in a successful manner. When you have a failure, it is because you have not asked for enough. Keep on and a larger thing than what you were formerly seeking will certainly come to you.

Disappointment Is Just an Adjustment

Disappointment may appear when things don't happen as fast as you would you like them to or in just the way you want them to happen. Because your dream isn't quite perfect yet, you may be tempted to think it hasn't actually arrived!

When you build dreams, expect needs for adjustments, somewhat like adjustments a sports team makes at halftime. Make creative adjustments as the dream materializes.

My dream was to move to the beach in California. When the opportunity came, I moved to California. As I spent time there, I found specific things I liked and disliked. I was grateful to be near the beach, a dream come true! Yet, I found that in building my ideal home in my dreams, there is nowhere in California to house that dream. California is noisy and crowded, with a train running near the beach blaring its horn every few hours!

I have adjusted my dream of the ideal home. My refined dream is for a home in Hawaii. Hawaiian beaches have the same qualities as California beaches, but the climate is warmer and we can grow fruit trees. The view and its ambiance will be absent of train lines that run next to the beach all the way up the California Coast. This was not a detail I knew about until my dream began to materialize! We keep making adjustments to our dreams, and we enjoy the parts of them that work.

Thoughts Become Things

When you catch yourself engaged in thinking negative thoughts, convert them into adjustments to your dreams. Do not try to get rid of negative thoughts. Do not ignore or deny them (like the earlier example of not thinking of the pink elephant!). Remembering that thoughts become things, realize the importance of keeping your thoughts focused on what you want, not on what you DON'T want! Your awareness of fears, doubts, and disappointments is the key to realigning your focus on what you do want.

Negative thoughts and feelings are trying to speak to you. You may need to readjust your negative thinking, clear out some old destructive beliefs, and find an attitude of gratitude, or restructure your dream. These thoughts are symptoms. Look inside them for the message.

KEY POINTS TO REMEMBER

1. The difference in "failure" and success is in attitude.
2. Appearance is a distraction from your focus.
3. Stay focused on your big picture, on your dream.
4. Make stepping-stones of so-called disappointment.
5. Adjustments to dreams are part of the process.

POWER STUDY FOR COUNTER INTENTION

Dreams Alive by Paul Bauer, Secrets of Manifesting.

Website: www.dreamsalive.com.

[5.] Paul Bauer, *Dreams Alive: Secrets of Manifesting Action Series,* 2007.

Chapter 8

Build a Foundation of Faith

"Faith is to believe what you do not see; the reward of this faith is to see what you believe."
> –Saint Augustine

Faith and Religion

WHEN I USE such words as faith, truth, freedom, and other spiritual words, I do not mean them in a religious way. Religions are personal ways of expressing faith and belief in a higher power, a source, or a Creator.

That higher power has many names, even in The Bible. There are endless debates about which religion knows who God is, and who gets to name Him. However, for our purposes here, God is Creator, whatever His name . . . generically speaking. And for those who do not believe in an external god; please feel free to substitute the concept of God with your concept of inner self or inner strength.

Brand of Faith

The brand of faith we use in the *author your reality* process is less important than trusting and believing in ourselves.

What brand of milk do you drink? It's a personal preference, yet it is still milk. What kind of car do you drive, Ford, Chevy, or Mercedes? No matter the kind of car, it's still a car and still needs gas to get from point A to point B. When I use words such as "faith" and "truth" and "God" and "reality," understand that I use them in the broadest, most generic sense; with faith being the gas that runs the religion you've selected for honoring your creator. For those who do not subscribe to an external creator you will trust the omnipresence within you to guide you on this journey.

What Is Faith? Who Is God?

Each March, I share a hotel room with a friend and colleague at a yearly business convention. She is Orthodox Jewish. Rachel wakes each morning before sunrise to pray, and eats only kosher meals. She exudes a centered confidence, punctuated by a strong sense of peace and joy. It is obvious that she loves her God with all her heart.I love my Lord with all my heart. She and I hold that love for God in common.

This year, after a long day on the show floor, the moment arrived for the sandwiches Rachel had thoughtfully prepared earlier. Exhausted, we plopped down on the steps of the Venetian in front of the "Venetian Canal" in Las Vegas. Hungry and chilled from the air conditioning inside, we gobbled down the kosher sandwiches and basked in the warm golden sunlight as the sun sank into the horizon behind the buildings. People were walking, talking, laughing, cussing; cars were honking and sirens blaring on a typical, hectic "Sin City" day.

Yet in an unexpected sudden, single, powerful eternal instant, the world stopped. The busy, crazy, noisy world became motionless, peaceful, and silent. We sat immersed in our separate meditations. Then, spontaneously, we looked up at one another. Unexpectedly, we caught each other's peaceful, joyful expression. That was a beautiful moment as we both became aware of sharing God's powerful presence in our midst—and each glimpsed tears of joy running down the other's face.

I might have felt vulnerable, except she was present in the same exact God-moment! We hugged each other in love and appreciation of sharing that unforgettably blessed moment, accompanied with joyful tears. Was it the kosher sandwich giving us the joy of that moment? I think not—as we have experienced other "God moments" without the sandwich, including such a moment with a Muslim Las Vegas cab driver who clearly loves his understanding of whom God is, as much as we love ours.

How blasphemous each of our individual dogmas would say we are—loving and sharing the same God-moment while passing on the claim to name that moment as exclusively originating from his or her religion. Yet this is what I call true generic faith—faith beyond religions, faith in a power and being greater and more loving, more knowing than we are. It is a faith in a God so big and so all encompassing it cannot be adequately described by one single name!

Generic Faith

No religion has ownership of the present moment. Faith beyond a brand of religion is the understanding of that powerful omnipresence of the present moment. How glorious to experience and receive that powerful, loving, truth into your personal space.

Yet, how often do we experience this powerful presence of God?

Many of us spend our entire lives chasing God's presence, when it's right there as close as our breath, right under our noses.

Yet not recognizing it, many try to fill the void with drugs, music, money, work, status, religion, and fame. We have a god-void—a faith void. Generic faith is receiving and recognizing the power, peace, and joy; of that all-knowing, all-powerful, all-loving Omnipresence—right here in the present moment.

We can apply the power of faith to attract our dreams into our present time and place! How do we tap into that power? How do we live in faith? We march right into the present moment, act in the present moment, receive the present moment, and practice thankfulness for the present moment, just as it is!

Distractions from the Present Moment

Why does it seem so difficult to achieve harmony with the present moment, to be and live and function in the present moment? If it is right here and now, why does it seem to elude us? There are so many distractions from the truth of the present moment. Honest faith is what snaps us right back into the present moment.

False Faith and Honest Faith

How will we know if we are experiencing false faith or honest faith? Honest faith is characterized by trusting in the present moment. False faith is characterized by a feeling about the future or the past. When dwelling on the past, you are working from your weakest position.

Faith Is the Attractor of Your Dreams

"Fake it until you make it!" We have all heard that, but I honestly believe that faking it isn't going to make it! In order to attract our real desires and our real dreams, we need to get real. Once we do get real, we discover our true desires, passions, talents, and courageously admit what they are. We begin to walk in true faith; truly trusting ourselves and our inner creativity.

"Faking it until you make it," does have a grain of truth to it. But if you are faking your journey, then you must realize that your desires are appearance motivated, rather than coming from your deepest, inner desires. To bring out your deepest and truest desires and passions requires real and honest soul searching, and faking this part isn't going to make it.

Therefore, stay in the present moment and be aware of the difference between the "fake" and "real" faith. The fake will drain and real faith will sustain! If we are operating on a competitive realm and ego level, our faith in who we are and in what our true purpose is will be hidden by who we are trying to please, and the appearance of what we are trying to become. In that realm we will not tune in to abundance, rather we will struggle in competitive mode where there *isn't enough*. And where there *"isn't enough,"* there *isn't enough* real faith, either.

Your Published Vision Book

We have provided incredible tools in the *Author Your Reality Action Plan*. First is this book, and the companion workbook, and most important part of this self-development course is your published *vision book*.

Trust that you are experiencing the Omnipresence right now. When you start to catch yourself in doubt, fear, worry, or counter intention, pull out the book authored by you, with your pictures, words, thoughts, drawings, images, numbers, and timeline all wrapped up in your published vision book. Review it, read it, feel it, believe it, receive, and achieve it.

KEY POINTS TO REMEMBER

1. Distinguish between religious and generic faith.
2. Cultivate your relationship with your Creator, or Omnipresence.
3. Faith is your awareness of God's presence right now.
4. Stay in God's presence.
5. Real faith and self-trust is the attractor of your dreams.

POWER STUDY FOR FAITH

The Theory of Reality: Learn Quickly and Easily How to Change Your Life and Live Your Dream[1]. Larry and Diana Bogartz, published by Xlibris Corporation. This is a great book about faith as related to creating reality, with and techniques for building and practicing faith.

Website: www.theoryofreality.com

Chapter 9

Energy, Entropy, Momentum

"The visible world is the invisible organization of energy."
—Physicist Heinz Paz

Faith Plus Energy Equals Momentum

Our energy level builds on faith in God and/or trust in self to generate magnetism and vibrational force, which attracts visualizations. This chapter addresses the energy needed to fuel our dreams. Get ready to rev up your energy level to spark up your dream.

The Basic Law of Entropy

The law of entropy applied to general conditions refers to the propensity of things, if left alone, to dissipate or deteriorate.

David Hawkins' Map of Consciousness

Dr. David Hawkins has done some interesting research, which measures energy vibration to associate the measurements with emotional and/or spiritual states. Whether the figures below are exact, or the order correct, Dr. David Hawkins' research proves the premise that we vibrate at spiritual and emotional energy levels, which he has measured as follows:

Enlightenment	700-1000
Peace	600
Joy	550
Love	500
Reason	400
Acceptance	300
Willingness	310
Neutrality	240
Courage	200
Pride	170
Anger	150
Desire	125
Fear	100
Grief	75
Apathy	50
Guilt	30

The Law of Entropy applied to personal energy levels gives clues about how to energize our dreams. If we express the lower numbered emotions with regard to our goals and dreams, we can expect entropy. Our dreams can literally dry up in front of our eyes.

As we build and sustain generic faith while visualizing our dream, we create momentum for our dream by investing energy in that dream. Invest higher-level energies as indicated by this chart, or invest in states that you determine will build the highest energy for you.

One category Hawkins may have overlooked is gratitude. I would place gratitude at 650, because I have experienced it as one of my higher energy states.

Invest Energy to Create Dream Momentum

The workbook will guide you to rate your states. You will identify states that enhance energy and those that subtract from it. To the extent that you spend energy on states not enhancing to your well being, you delete energy from the opportunity to conceive, believe, receive, and achieve your dream.

Build Self-Energy

We have come to understand the value of self-esteem, which is key to the *author your reality* process. Equally important is to develop what I term as "self-energy." Self-energy can be cultivated in many ways.

Physical Energy

At a basic physical level, we run on sleep, food, air, and water. Dedicate some time each day to building the quality of these elements. Once your dreams are activated, physical stamina and health will allow for full enjoyment. Give yourself the highest quality water, food, sleep, and air on a daily basis. Your dreams require it! For example, if you dream of traveling to Europe, the situation will require extensive walking; and preparing yourself to receive this dream will involve getting into excellent walking condition.

Be generous with yourself with sleep, good food, and exercise. Once your dream comes towards you, you will want your physical condition to be at its best, in order to receive the dream via your inspired action.

Brain Energy

Dr. Daniel G. Amen is teaching a new health care—that of taking care of the brain. As a proponent of brain health, his clinic addresses chronic and common brain dysfunction issues including ADD, ADHD, drug dependence, depression, bipolar disease, dementia, and Alzheimer's disease. His work also includes teaching about the prevention of brain dysfunctions through the use of natural remedies and by avoiding substance abuse. He also stresses the importance of proactively exercising the body and brain for maximum oxygen and maximum overall health. He believes that if the brain is functioning well, the body will function well, too. Your deepest and truest desires and passions require real and honest soul searching, and faking this part isn't going to make it.

Reactionary Energy

We choose our reaction to any given situation. This explains why some successful people come from the humblest of backgrounds, while some unsuccessful people come from advantageous backgrounds.

Consciously choosing "the attitude of gratitude" provides maximum energy to feel good about our day. Feeling good builds self-energy! Whining, complaining, and reacting negatively causes self-energy leakage! Be aware of emotional energy drains and attempt to substitute those negative emotions with emotions of acceptance, peace, or gratitude when faced with frustrating or difficult situations.

I am not referring to a denial of what is—which would be energy draining. Rather, I suggest that you make a conscious choice about how to react is energy building! Your moment-by-moment choice is between building self-energy and subtracting from it. In order to receive dreams that you envision, build up strong self-energy through your emotional expressions and reactions.

Spiritual Energy

Equally important is the simple, but not always easy, practice of spending time with your source. Spending time alone with your Creator is a source of inspiration and energy. Getting still in prayer or meditation creates a bond with your Creator and allows a powerful flow of communication, inspiration, and creativity—the critical raw materials of dream building.

Love Energy

Investing energy in those whom you love and those who love you, as you are, brings amazing returns. When you are truly in love and involved in healthy, loving, balanced relationships, the appreciation, joy, and peace inspire immeasurable energy from and to your core. Healthy relationships are balanced. You will not feel resentful, angry, or cheated. Some friends, family, and lovers should have limited attention from you because of the energy drain they create. This doesn't mean you forget them forever; only that they are not in the time or place where a healthy exchange of love energy is possible.

Tough Love Energy

Many books cover the subject of healthy relationships, but the basic principle we apply is "tough love." Tough love insists that we are honored for who we are within the relationship. Accept it when someone is not able to honor you as you honor him or her. They may be involved with an addiction or other energy—draining challenges. They are learning the value of negativity by intensely experiencing it on a daily basis. They will be a drain on you, if you let them.

You may love them from a distance, but do not allow them to impede your progress toward becoming a growing, loving person who is following your dreams.

Once they see you living your dreams, you will become the inspiration for them to live their dreams. Limit the amount of friction you allow loved ones to impose upon you in the name of love. Teach those you love to honor your highest aspirations by creating distance when they refuse to do so.

Personal Development Energy

The best investments you make are in yourself, and in loved ones. True, you won't see a regular paycheck right away, but there is a generous payoff which is way beyond any false sense of security. How would you know this? Take a risk and invest in yourself—personally, spiritually, and professionally.

Momentum Energy

Frances Willard said, "I would not waste my life in friction when it could be turned to momentum." Momentum is the spinning force that makes things happen, you invest energy until it emits such a force that it creates a life of its own. This happens when you generate self-energy and invest it in a dream. Daily increments of faith, energy, and inspired action bring the dream alive. You control the momentum to rev up your energy level to conceive, believe, receive, and achieve your dream.

KEY POINTS TO REMEMBER

1. Faith plus energy equals momentum.
2. Law of Entropy—energy dissipates if left unattended.
3. Pass up friction energy when you recognize it.
4. Invest in yourself—energy and your self-development.
5. Momentum spins itself into the dream.

POWER STUDY TO MAXIMIZE PERSONAL ENERGY

Power vs. Force, the Hidden Determinants of Human Behavior, by Dr. David Hawkins, M.D. PhD.

Website: www.veritaspub.com

Chapter 10

Your Mind's Eye

"Visualize this thing that you want, see it, feel it, believe in it. Make your mental blue print, and begin to build."
—Robert Collier

Forming the Dream-Vision

FORMULATING AN IDEA in your mind's eye is critical in bringing your dreams to life. This is where many of us get stuck. This is because we haven't quite figured out how to bring the desire, the passion, the dream, to our mind's eye! Let's explore something enlightening about you. How do you best express yourself? Are you visual, auditory, kinesthetic, or cerebral?

The Visual Approach

People who are primarily visually oriented can formulate their vision by closing their eyes and picturing a scene or event. These people enjoy movies, film, design, art, color, photos, form, beauty, and symmetry. When they understand something they may say, "I see what you mean."

Their favorite game is probably a card game—bridge or poker. When recalling people, they will remember the person's face. When picturing a waterfall in Hawaii, they might intensely imagine the white, misty spray of the water as it tumbles down the steep mountainside contrasted with the beauty of the deep green foliage in the lush, tropical forest.

The Auditory/Verbal Approach

People who are primarily auditory enjoy music, rhythm, singing, listening to books on tape, talking on the phone, writing, reading, telling stories, word games, crossword puzzles. They tend to be verbal, and when they understand something they might say, "I *hear* what you're saying!" Their favorite game could be Scrabble or crossword puzzles. When it comes to people, they remember names easily. When imagining a waterfall in Hawaii, the deafening sound of the powerful crashing water hitting hard rocks at the bottom will be the overwhelming interest and attraction in their mind's eye.

Kinesthetic Movers and Shakers

People who are oriented kinesthetically tend to be physical and sensual. They may gravitate towards being athletes, actors, preachers, and politicians. They are passionate, hyperactive, and three-dimensional. They like dancing, skiing, rocking, running, flying, moving, jumping, tapping, squirming, climbing, balancing, and traveling.

Of course, kinesthetic people will tend to be gregarious, the life of the party, and they know lots of people. They enjoy emotion, are energized by contact with people, and might tend towards the dramatic. Motivated by feelings, when they understand something, they might say, "I *feel* you." Their favorite game might be Twister, and when remembering people, they will remember the person's sun sign before they recall their name or face. When imagining a waterfall in Hawaii, they might imagine themselves in a helicopter flying over, or whitewater rafting in a kayak below the falls.

Cerebral Type

If you are cerebral, you will tend to use your mind to figure things out, aided by your sense of logic. You will enjoy a strong sense of discipline, and employ study, techniques, research, questions, and systems to further your goals. Your way of remembering people is something that you have disciplined yourself to do over time because you know it's important. Your favorite game may be chess, and you are adept on the computer and great at remembering names and faces.

You have a legal and technical mind, and will tend to be motivated by "what you believe is right." When you understand something, you will say, "I *think* I know what you mean!" If you are a cerebral type, your vision of the waterfall in Hawaii may include a close-up view to question, scrutinize, and compare the environmental or geographical effects of the grinding power of the water.

Identifying your Expressive Style

Start watching yourself in order to identify your main expressive style. Of course, all of us use all four styles, but lean towards one style or another. Understanding your style will help you choose a primary method for formulating your dream to bring it to reality. And you won't feel like a failure if you aren't particularly excited about one type of expressive style.

If you are visually oriented, you probably own a pretty cool digital camera, which means you will be an excellent candidate for taking your own photos for your *published vision book*. Start thinking about photos to take that will stimulate, inspire, and complete your vision. Your own personal photos are going to have a great impact on your subconscious mind, which will subtly attract what you want.

If you are auditory or verbal, start collecting poetry and quotes, and begin writing bits and pieces of inspiration that mean something to you. You probably already have a journal and can pull some of your most exciting words from that. You may also already have some poetry. Because you are auditory, you love putting words together for effective creative expression.

If you are kinesthetic, you can start building your dream with feelings and movement. A theme, a moral, a story will form for you, and you will find a script developing, which you may embellish with photos, art, and words.

If you are cerebral, you may want to outline your dream and the steps needed to achieve it. Your *published vision book* may look like a storyboard, or a Power Point slide show. Whatever way you best express yourself is the best way to put together elements in order to build and create your *published vision book.*

Collect Script Elements

If you are primarily visual, begin to collect pictures and photos, if you are auditory, you will want to collect music, songs, poetry, and quotes. And, if you are kinesthetic, you may want to journal your feelings, impressions, thoughts on your ideal home, love relationship, physical body, vacation, or career change. If you are cerebral, you may fill in the details of your outline.

Define a Dream

Take a look at your photos, quotes, journaling, and rational conclusions; and choose an idea of something you have always wanted to do or become. Keep it simple, and later you can manifest bigger dreams. Write it down and speak it to yourself. This is the first step in writing your dream script for your published *vision book.* Write it in the present tense, "I learn to surf." "I take a month—long vacation to Italy." "I take the exam for my real estate license, (remodel the kitchen, ask for a raise, learn to play a musical instrument, or speak a foreign language)." *The workbook* gives you ideas to stimulate your imagination and help you select a dream that will excite you.

Preparing Your Dream Story

Develop awareness of your predominate style of visualizing and begin to collect dream elements using your favorite expressive style. You can easily move forward in creative visualization even if you aren't someone who is good at visualizing pictures in your mind. The idea is to transform your dreams into a form that you may naturally practice imagining. Whether that form is pictures, words, feelings, or thoughts, you will be most successful once you find your best medium of expression of visualization!

KEY POINTS TO REMEMBER

1. Different people exhibit different expression styles.
2. To give form to your dream you will give it expression.
3. Find your style: visual, auditory, kinesthetic, cerebral.
4. Collect script elements to ignite desires and passions.
5. Select a simple dream and write it in the present.

POWER STUDY ABOUT VISUALIZATION

Creative Visualization, by Shakti Gawain. A simple book on how to activate imagination and visualization in a purposeful way.

Website: www.shaktigawain.com.

The Way They Learn, Cynthia Ulrich Tobias, published by Focus on the Family, 1998.

Website: www.applest.com

PART THREE
RECEIVE

Chapter 11

Activate the Thinking Stuff

> "There is a thinking stuff from which all things are made. A thought in this substance, produces the thing that is imaged by the thought."
>
> —Wallace D. Wattles

Formulating your Dream Script

IN THIS CHAPTER we ask you to gather the components for your dream script. There will be a storyline to your dream script that includes a beginning, middle, and an end. Depending on whether you are primarily visual, auditory, kinesthetic, or cerebral, you will collect various components to represent your desirable dream outcome.

The Thinking Stuff

In Chapter Four we spoke of the thinking stuff, and this is the ethereal stuff, or "the field," into which our dreams are planted, shaped, and formed. Wallace D. Wattles writes:

"There is a thinking stuff from which all things are made, and which, in its original state, permeates, penetrates, and fills the interspaces of the universe. A thought in this substance produces the thing that is imaged by the thought. A person can form things in his thought, and, by impressing his thought upon formless substance, can cause the thing he thinks about to be created."

Transforming Desires to Physical Reality

This is where the rubber meets the road, and the end of the road for many, coming to a dead-end with desires stuck in a cul-de-sac of fantasy! However, using the tool of *The Published Vision Book,* we actively move past the fantasy to the reality!

Last chapter we addressed the four different styles of expression: visual, auditory/verbal, kinesthetic, and cerebral. The reason we did this is so you could determine your most predominate style of expression.

Activating Inspiration and Desire

Remember, in Chapter 1 I asked you to bring your courage with you? Although courage is the inspiration that brings your dreams into reality, courage can be frightening. This is because we find ourselves not knowing or not being able to decide on a dream. We cannot see it, feel it, speak of it, or think of it. Therefore, I am going to make some suggestions as to how you can stimulate the creative genius inside of you.

Shopping Trip

This is a great method for the kinesthetic or the visually expressive person. If you are dreaming of a new car, go test-drive it, if you want to remodel your kitchen, go to kitchen design studios to look at possible designs and treatments. Bring a camera and take photos of those ideas or objects that appeal to you. Collect and incorporate them into your dream script, which will ultimately become your *published vision book.*

Movies and Music

Invest a few bucks in your favorite movie or music to stimulate something you want to create for yourself. If your dream is to become an athlete or to perfect yourself in a certain sport, or to travel to an exotic or far away place, renting or buying an appropriate movie will inspire you and give you ideas for elements to collect for your dream script.

Your dream script is going to be the story about how you are experiencing the dream because you will write your *vision book* in the powerful present tense. This is why we look for little ways to begin experiencing the dream.

If you are thinking of becoming a lawyer, rent movies or read books about some of the most incredible legal stories and lawsuits in history.

Books and Research

If you are the cerebral type, you will enjoy researching the subject of your desire. Go to the library, check out books or go to a bookstore for information on the specific subject that you love. If you have decided you want to learn how to surf, get some books, go to a place that gives lessons, find out about your local adult education classes, go on the Internet and gather all the information you can for the vision plan you are preparing to write and publish.

Field Trips

Field trips are a great way to begin to experience your dream. One of my dreams is to be able to afford to go out to the most exclusive and beautiful restaurants. I love the ambiance and environment of being at dinner with candles, or enjoying lunch at an outdoor table overlooking the ocean.

One of my field trips involved going to a five-star resort restaurant overlooking one of the most beautiful beaches in California. How did I afford it? I went to lunch, not dinner, and

I bought the least expensive thing on the menu, and drank only water.

It was *the* most expensive hamburger I have ever eaten! It was fabulous! I was treated like a queen, was able to take about two hours soaking up the sun and the view, and watching rich and famous people coming and going in the restaurant. It only cost me $25, and it gave me the flavor and feeling of beauty, elegance, and abundance.

I skipped my next three fast food meals to make up for the money spent on that meal, but now I have increased my vision level and have invested in the dream of treating myself well.

There are botanical gardens, rose gardens, zoos, castles, art galleries, businesses, museums, and all kinds of field trips you can take to bring your imagination alive in the area of your passion. Bring your digital camera so that you may take photos to include in your *published vision book*.

Interviews

If your dream is to become a writer, athlete, or attorney, do some research to find a successful local professional in that field. Most people, when approached properly, enjoy sharing and talking about their successes with those who admire them.

It won't need to be someone incredibly famous, but rather someone working full time in your field of interest. This will help you "try on" the dream, and bring it to life. It will stimulate your thinking to a level that will help you formulate how you are going to want to live the dream of working in that career or profession.

If your dream is to travel abroad, visit the local embassy of your favorite country. Locate a local grocery store that stocks the food of that region to start buying and cooking food from that region. In addition to buying groceries, visit or chat with the people who work there who may have inside information about the country you wish to visit.

Bringing it All Together

Now that you have gone on field trips, interviews, researched, read books, and gone to movies, you are ready to write your dream statement. You will have specifics about your dream to include shapes, colors, flavors, and you will have increased your desire, hope, and passion for the dream. Write your dream statement in *The workbook* in 15 words or less. Phrase it in the present. "I am a best-selling, non-fiction author in the area of entrepreneurialism." If so inspired, you may write and illustrate how you are going to go about living in the middle of your dream. When you begin to put together your *published vision book, the workbook* will explain how to use the software to import illustrations and your dream statement.

Select a strong visual image for your cover and write a summary of the story of your dream as if already done. When writing your dream script, keep in mind you are speaking to your inner subconscious; therefore speak, in the present tense in a positive tone, always stating what you want. This is critical because whatever you focus on, you get. Be certain to write, picture, and feel what you *want—not* what you *don't want*.

The Workbook for the Author Your Reality Action Plan

The workbook will walk you through the self-publishing software to create your *published vision book*. The vision book format is a 7 x 7 full-color 10 to 40-page storybook. There is no pressure to fill up pages, but as you practice your dream with interviews, field trips, movies, music, books, and research, you will get many ideas. It will be easy to fill the pages.

KEY POINTS TO REMEMBER

1. Activating your desires and dreams takes courage.
2. Activating your desires and dreams requires action.
3. Test dreams with field trips, interviews, films, books.

4. Write your dream statement in 15 words or less.
5. Use the book publishing software to put it together for you.

POWER STUDY FOR DECIDING TO DREAM

The Power of Intention, by Dr. Wayne W. Dyer Hay House, Inc., Carlsbad, California. This book is about the harnessing the power of what you strongly desire to bring into reality. Dr. Wayne W Dyer speaks of "intent" as a way of focusing desire into activity and building momemtum towards your desired outcome.

Website: www.drwaynedyer.com

Chapter 12

Ten Dream Steps for Success

"The truth dazzles gradually, else the world would be blind."

–Emily Dickinson

Putting Power in Your Dream Steps

IN ORDER TO come from power, a clear understanding of the past, present, and future is critical. The past is gone and is but a dim memory. In dwelling on the past, we can be deterred from our dreams, dream scripts, and dream objectives. By emotionally living in the past, we distract ourselves from discovering and giving voice to our deepest, most inspirational desires.

The Past Does not Equal the Future

In pointing to the past, we stir up negative explanations as to why our dreams can't come true and it's because they haven't come true in the past. It is a specific sort of blame game and subtracts from our power to take responsibility for what our life has become. Develop a powerful habit of catching yourself in these thoughts and instantly correct them by shifting your power to take direct action in the present moment.

Our lives are a reflection of what we continuously focus on. Therefore, if we continue to focus on what happened in the past, we continue to repeat the past. History repeats itself, particularly for those who keep focusing on it!

"But how can I learn from my mistakes if I don't look back?" Although this question seems to make sense, there is a weakness in this thinking. It makes the assumption that mistakes have been made. If we go back to Chapter Seven, we learned that there is no such thing as failure, and that all seeming failure is an opportunity for adjustment and in many cases, attitude adjustments. An adjustment is an improvement, rather than a correction of a mistake. When we think in terms of mistakes, this thinking comes from lack or fear.

In thinking from power, faith, and responsibility, we simply, constantly make improvements. When we shift our thinking from fear of repeating mistakes to acceptance of a learning opportunity, the negative past loses its power over us.

The Future

The future is exciting because it's a blank slate, and as long as we see it as a creative opportunity, the future will not keep us in fear. The reality is that the past is gone and the future is not yet here, so by investing ourselves too much in either the past or the future, we diminish our power to act in the present moment.

If we try to live in the future in our mind, then we can easily get into fear, and become afraid of what will or won't happen. "What if?" may be a statement of fear about the future, and when you catch yourself saying it, that is an opportunity to change your attitude to one of faith instead of fear.

Having faith in the future is a way to establish your dreams in the thinking stuff. Fear of the future is focusing on and visualizing a negative outcome. To see good dreams manifested, invest positive faith in the future and guide your thoughts away from fear of the future and fear of the past.

The Powerful Present Moment

The past and future are illusory. They are not tangible, and only reside in the mind. This is where the self-control of thoughts can influence your dreams—in the present moment. The present moment is so powerful that modern quantum physics shows evidence that the present can alter the past. When we begin to define our dream statement of 15 words or less, it is powerful to make the statement in the present tense. We, therefore, visualize our dreams in the present and can actually attract the future based on our focus.

The Ten Steps for Success from *Author Your Reality Workbook*

STEP 1 — **Launch Your Courage**
CONCEPT: Courage to Dream

STEP 2 — **Drive Your Desires**
CONCEPT: Conscious Belief Systems

STEP 3 — **Free Your Imagination**
CONCEPT: Imagination Stimulation

STEP 4 — **Stage Your Dream**
CONCEPT: Enlightened Visualization

STEP 5 — **Pen Your Dream Script**
CONCEPT: Power of Words-Write it!

STEP 6 — **Set Your Dream on Fire**
CONCEPT: Ignite Dream Momentum

STEP 7 — **Publish Your Published Vision Book**
CONCEPT: Connect with the "Thinking Stuff"

STEP 8 — **Inspire Your Dream with Action**
CONCEPT: Power of the Present Moment

STEP 9 — **Awaken Your Dream with Thanks**
CONCEPT: Attraction Action of Gratitude

STEP 10— **Become a Dream Achiever**
CONCEPT: Live, Share, Expand Your Dreams

KEY POINTS TO REMEMBER

1. The past is past and has no power over you.
2. The past does not have to equal the future.
3. The powerful present is the only place to take action.
4. Use faith to plant dreams into "the thinking stuff."
5. Use *the workbook* to learn dream steps one by one.

POWER STUDY FOR TAKING THE DREAM STEPS

Author Your Reality Action Plan Workbook, by Deborah S. Nelson. Published, DS Publishing CO, September 2012.

Website: www.authoryourdreams.com

Chapter 13

Receive Your Dream

> "Sometimes I've believed as many as six impossible things before breakfast."
>
> –Lewis Carroll

When the Dream Arrives

YOUR DREAM WILL enter the atmosphere of your life in bits and pieces. Be prepared to welcome its arrival on your scene. Ignore it, and it may crash and burn before it gets to you. Resist the temptation to look for it and then conclude that it hasn't arrived. Instead, look expectantly for evidences of its appearance, and make note of those things that you are attracting.

Now that I am living in California (a dream come true), one of my latest dreams is to upgrade my Lexus to a newer model Mercedes Benz convertible. My girlfriend and I went to drive one at the local dealership and it was fabulous!

Recently, I received an unexpected call from a longtime friend completely "out of the blue." He told me about an opportunity to buy (for himself) a convertible Mercedes Benz for an amazing price. He wanted to park it in my driveway as well as let me drive it for a time. His present neighborhood was too rough to accommodate the car without the risk of being stolen.

For a number of reasons, I decided not to participate in the opportunity, but I am excited and encouraged to see that my convertible Mercedes Benz is starting to break through to my atmosphere, and it is on its way!

Practicing Gratitude

A critical component for receiving your dream is to practice thankfulness. Cultivating this state of mind brings you closer to your Creator. It also brings you to the position where you can see and accept the pieces of the puzzle that will make up your dream. Being thankful allows you to tune into the events being attracted into your life, and thankfulness also gives you the opportunity to receive and accept the things that will lead you to the realization of your dreams.

Balance Expectation with Faith

Planting a dream into the "Thinking Stuff" is similar to planting a seed in the ground. "Water" it daily by reading it, looking at it, conceptualizing it, reciting it, or feeling it as already done. As the days, weeks, months, and years go by, you can expect the pieces of your dream story to come together as you nurture it with a beautiful blend of faith, visualization, expectation, and thankfulness.

Receive the Dream

To receive the dream is to recognize opportunities that have been attracted to you for realizing your dream. You will have many choices in "realizing your dream." You see the dream coming toward you and you decide you didn't really want it after all. In your mind and in your fantasy, you thought you wanted the dream, but living it doesn't seem so much fun after all.

This is perfectly acceptable. Sometimes we try on our dreams and they don't suit us. They don't quite fit. At that point, you may decide to turn down your dream. This need not be a disappointment or a failure, but a powerful choice. You can also readjust the dream.

Perhaps that beautiful, perfect car came into your life, but now you think or feel that the car payments are too stressful. It's the perfect car, you have the down payment, your credit has been approved, but all of a sudden, those payments don't feel quite right.

So you make an adjustment to your dream. You decide on a car a few years older for which you can trade your current automobile. You use it as your down payment, add some cash, and pay upfront for the used car of your dreams, with no car payments. As you receive your dream, make appropriate adjustments so that your dream feels just right for you!

Try on Your Dream

As you attract the dream toward you, and you see the pieces coming together, the way it enters the atmosphere of your reality may be a little different than the way you expected. Try on the dream. If you don't like it you can turn it down, or make some adjustments.

It's like trying on clothing. You pick out some stuff in your size that looks great on the rack, but you are never quite sure how it's going to look, fit, or feel until you try it on, and look at yourself in the mirror. Does the dream you have attracted actually fit? Or was it a superficial dream that you only *thought* you wanted?

What do you *really* want? You think you want money, when what you really want is the feeling of security. We want a relationship, when what we need is to learn how to love ourselves. We want a new job, when what we really need is self-employment. Look deep inside when you begin to try on your dreams to determine if you need to go back to the drawing board, readjust your attitude, or receive the dream coming to you with open arms and unwavering gratitude.

Gratitude and Courage

If you like what you see as your dream approaches, just liking it is an incredible catalyst to inspire thankfulness. You will have the opportunity to activate your dream by putting your stamp of approval on it. Everything that conspires to fulfill your dreams—the universe, God, or your source—will keep it coming as long as you courageously accept that you are worthy! The response of courage and thankfulness sets the stage for the opportunity to receive your dream by taking *inspired action.*

Inspired Action

There is a world of difference between *inspired action* and disciplined action. Disciplined action is what we *make ourselves* do in response to external expectations, whereas inspired action is what pulls us intuitively and internally. It feels as if an invisible force is *pulling you* rather than *you pushing it*. If you are taking action based on what you think you "should do," or if you are trying to impress others or please them, this is a clue that the action you are about to take is from discipline.

Discipline will create apparent results, but *inspired action* comes from that to which you are strongly and passionately drawn towards. You will not have to make yourself do it, other than to overcome fear or limitations. Inspired action is nearly effortless; it's almost magical.

Activating Your Dream

Often inspired action will be required as an immediate response to an opportunity.

A few years ago, just before my daughter was to begin college, I was dreaming about how to do the impossible. How was I going to put her through a top-notch college, costing more than what I made as a yearly income? Yet, once my daughter and myself set our vision, we were undaunted.

Shortly before college was to begin, a part-time business opportunity was presented to me in an unexpected way. At the time, I was behind in my mortgage payment (any of you ever been there?) and when this opportunity came along, I found myself inspired to action!

In faith and with courage, I used half of the mortgage payment I had in hand to invest in this part time business opportunity. Within two weeks I had earned both mortgage payments owed. That part time business paid my daughter's $650-a-month rent for the entire duration of her college career. We will always be grateful for Pre-Paid Legal Services membership, and the business opportunity, which provided the extra cash flow, and affordable legal service as well.

All the Ingredients

Once the opportunity presented itself, I saw the vehicle for making our dream come true and we received the dream! It took a leap of faith fueled by a vision and an investment of action. This was a dream with many parts, and covering the large expense of a place for my daughter to live was a huge component that allowed us to get started in making her college dream come true! Before that moment, it was difficult to see how we were going to do it. It took inspired action on an opportunity presented to activate the dream.

KEY POINTS TO REMEMBER

1. Observe dream elements entering "your atmosphere."
2. You can choose to receive or refuse dream parts.
3. You can make adjustments to alter your dream.
4. Receive your dream opportunity with thankfulness.
5. Activate your dream with inspired action.

POWER STUDY OF THE POWER OF THOUGHT

What the Bleep Do We Know? Documentary, February 2005.

Website: www.whatthebleep.com

This is a documentary interviewing scientists and their understanding of quantum physics and how we define reality. Quantum physics is now proving that the observer (of an object or event) actually influences that object or event. This science has stunning evidence that this influence is so powerful it can alter future outcomes as well as rewrite the past. Quantum physics is beginning to conclude that our reality is defined by how we observe it.

Chapter 14

The Practice of Gratitude

> "If the only prayer you said in your whole life was, 'thank you,' that would suffice."
>
> –Meister Eckhart

Staying the Course

RIGHT ABOUT NOW many of you are going to put down this book. It may seem as if this program is too complicated and too difficult. Yet, isn't this what we so often do when we are attempting to bring our dreams to pass? We get so close, yet so far away, because we get discouraged and quit right before the dream is about to come true! Why is that?

This is the exact time when we must stay on the course. There is a simple way to stop discouragement. You can cut it off right at the root. While it's a very simple solution, the challenging part is remembering to do it. This solution works to banish negativity and discouragement while building faith for the long haul. It is the *Practice of Gratitude*.

Whining and Murmuring and Complaining

When I was growing up, I learned that complaining was impolite. I developed the disciplined habit in my outer appearance of "not complaining." However, that did not stop the complaining that was going on inside! Later, as I grew away from my parents, the whining and complaining overcame the training and over time, I began complaining aloud again.

We can fake it by acting polite and classy and creating a wonderful and positive appearance, and that's nice. However, it doesn't get the job done for making dreams come true. This is where so many of us stumble. Yet, there is such an easy solution.

Spiritual Alchemy

The study of making your dreams come true may seem, at times, a little like the study of magic. But to live out our dreams is actually part of our true nature. Culture, society, and government continually feed us the message that only their institutions can help just a few special "star-types" to experience their dreams. The rest of us are destined to serve the bigger, more important dream. We are continually fed propaganda that to live out our dreams is somehow magical, miraculous, or rare, rather than to be informed and encouraged that living our dreams is actually our true nature!

If there is any magic in the process, it is in learning how to change the channel, shut out the propaganda, tune in to abundance, and receive the dream! If there is one magic trick in this whole process, thankfulness is it! Once we start to shift our attention to gratitude; everything around us begins to shine a lot more brightly.

Shifting from the Competitive by Using Gratitude

In the chapter on abundance, we covered competitive thinking versus creative thinking. Gratitude is the engine that keeps creative thinking on track. It is easy to be attracted by advertising, the words of co-workers, and the visions of others that lead us into the thinking that there is "not enough for me to be successful, too."

Once we start thinking and acting as if there is "not enough," only the people on top who are telling us there is "not enough" seem to "have enough." But truthfully, even they don't "have enough," because their vision is based on the competitive realm; which means it can always be taken away by someone younger, smarter, stronger, prettier, better, or just more competitive.

In the creative realm, we have access to the thinking stuff, and there is an unlimited amount of thinking stuff. There will always be "enough." "Enough" can always be created from the "thinking stuff." Keeping our mindset focused in the realm of the creative is difficult when we are living in a primarily competitive world. Those who are "on top" of the competitive world wield massive finances and power to keep the propaganda going—the lie that we are not good enough, smart enough, strong enough, pretty enough, and so on. That belief system keeps us on the treadmill of consuming and serving; not our own vision, but theirs.

OPV-Other People's Visions

To break this cycle of serving others' visions, we can practice thankfulness. Thankfulness brings power to our circumstances. Walking and breathing and thinking "thank you" is the antidote to negative thinking, the power of propaganda, and of getting sucked into the vortex of other people's visions.

There is nothing wrong with other people's visions, but to the extent you live in other people's visions, you become numb to your own vision and limit your ability to live out your dreams.

The Mind Spin, the Meltdown, the Panic

In the companion workbook, we show you how to dissolve "fear points" that continually try to assert themselves over your true desires. Once you begin to recognize these "familiar friends" in your thought processes, you will learn to apply thankfulness and appreciation to neutralize these fear points.

Thankfulness and gratitude are the most effective ways to change the channel of your mind. If you keep focusing on panic or meltdown, or letting your mind spin, you will rob your progress of energy, momentum, and vision.

The Magnifying Glass in the Grass

When I was a young girl, a fascinating toy I was given was a magnifying glass. We used it to focus light and energy to create heat on a blade of dry grass to start a campfire.

Originally, this was a Boy Scout trick. In order to make it work, you need to hold the magnifying glass perfectly still, and focus a ray of light on dry pieces of grass and twigs.

It took concentration, focus, and patience to take one form of energy and transform it into another (light burning grass). That's a small picture of what it takes to ignite your dream. When you find yourself at a place where you want to shift, or move, or give up, instead hold steady. Stay perfectly still in your desire to fire up your dream to a warm, crackling reality.

It takes a focused and sustained effort to bring about a dream. Practicing thankfulness, appreciation, and gratitude fans the flames of the desires and passions you hold dear. There may be a point where you want to squirm, move, shift, or give up, but stay still and stay focused just a little longer until you begin to see the smolder of smoke igniting the dry grass. As you feed the blaze with more grass, then twigs and kindling, eventually the fire will blaze. At that point, you can bring the dream alive with marshmallows, S'mores, and campfire songs. Then it will be time to have fun and enjoy your dream.

Thankfulness Is Attractiveness

Another benefit of thankfulness is its attraction. Like a laser beam of light, appreciation draws people, events, and circumstances to join you in the dream steps you are taking.

Due to circumstances in my family, I put myself through college. I was part of the work/study program and paid for the entire education myself. By the time I graduated, the bill was paid. My parents bought one set of books (about $220), I had a couple of small scholarships, and I finished without getting any student loans—my dream come true!

Why then would I be inspired to pay for another college education, that of my daughter's? Of all people, you would think that I would say, "Pay for it yourself!" Yet, even as a single mom, I paid for the majority of her college with cash as we went. The total cost was $150,000. She worked part time and took out small student loans, and she did her part. But whatever would possess me to be so dedicated as to pay for a second round of college education—hers?

It was her appreciation and thankfulness. Nothing else could have ever inspired me to put out the effort and the money.

How powerful it is when someone is truly thankful for what you do! Think how that makes you feel—the energy it brings and the purpose it provides. Quality people want to be around thankful people. Thankfulness is a powerful motivator, attractor, and stimulator. In your journey to make your dreams come true, apply the practice and the power of gratitude whenever you find your attitude, energy, or purpose faltering or slipping.

KEY POINTS TO REMEMBER

1. Stay on the course by employing gratitude.
2. Allow gratitude and spiritual alchemy to change your mindset.
3. Thankfulness is the antidote to fear, panic, and insecurity.
4. Appreciation attracts people, events to your dream.
5. Gratitude connects us to our source of life.

POWER STUDY OF THE POWER OF THOUGHT

The Astonishing Power of Gratitude; Wes Hooper.

Website: www.dailygratitude.com

There is a free PDF download of the book at the website. This book explains that the practice of gratitude is not only a basic spiritual principal, but that it can attract things of tremendous value to your sphere of influence.

Chapter 15

Be Careful What You Dream!
It might come true

"All that we are is the result of what we have thought. The mind is everything. What we think we become."
—Maharishi Mahesh Yogi

The Cinderella Story

THE CINDERELLA STORY is a fabulous story about dreaming! We typically think it is simply a love story, and while that is a legitimate interpretation, I have a different take.

Cinderella had a pretty bad attitude. She felt sorry for herself when she might have been thankful. Granted, her mother had died, and her father remarried. In her misery, she allowed her new sisters to make her into a slave and didn't stand up for herself. She was a martyr and enjoyed the drama of being a sad, grieving victim.

Cinderella hid her talent and beauty behind the sad state of affairs she had accepted. Eventually, she grew tired and started dreaming her way out of her bad attitude. She decided to take some risk. She dared to dream about going to the ball to meet the prince.

She dreamed big, and while her sisters were also vying to become the next queen, Cinderella's dream prevailed. She had mastered the skill of *authoring your reality*.

Bringing Author Your Reality Is a Skill Set

Once you learn the steps and the skills to bring your dreams to reality, take on bigger, better, and more complex dreams. We might find that the dream requires a little tweaking, some rewinding, or even major "halftime adjust merits." Be willing to look at your *published vision book* periodically to see how many of the dream pieces have entered your stage and how they are shaping into form.

It Didn't Go Quite that Way in My Mind

When your dream comes true, you suddenly have no excuses. There is no more feeling sorry for yourself, no more villains to blame, and no drama-adrenaline rush! You may even find your biochemistry expecting a "drama-fix!"

Sometimes, when a dream comes to pass, it doesn't feel quite right. It feels like something is missing—the longing, the seeking, the dissatisfaction, the excuses, and the blaming. All these things are missing, as we now have taken responsibility for making our dreams come true. It may feel as if you have lost an old friend, and often you *will* have lost some old friends.

When a dream comes true, you may find that you do not have the energy level to sustain the lifestyle of that dream come true. Those car payments are too high. Your husband is too clingy; the big home is too cold.

As our dreams come true, details fill in as living color! We can readjust our dreams—maybe a less macho man, a smaller car, a warmer home. Fine. We simply go back to the "drawing board" and rewrite the dream script. It's fine to try on dreams in a dress rehearsal to make the adjustments. We can edit our dreams as we see fit!

Don't Want What You Don't Want

A close friend, who is continuously pursuing his self-development, is quick to correct me when aspects of my dream don't show up as I expected. He says, "Don't want what you don't want."

In my frustration, I respond to him, "What? What do you mean? It's obvious that I don't want what I don't want!"

But he's trying to remind me of something. It's not turning out, as I "wanted" because there is an underlying purpose for it to be that way. All right then, my next question is, *Why wouldn't I want what I thought I wanted?*

This powerful question forces us to realize that if pieces of the dream haven't arrived as expected, there is opportunity for adjustment. We can take responsibility that our powerful subconscious created this scenario for a reason.

Keep On Dreaming—and Ask the Reason

Look deep inside to find out the possible reasons:

1. It's not your dream; someone else wanted it for you.
2. Your creative visualization was vague.
3. Limiting beliefs are blocking it.
4. Forgetting to receive the dream with thankfulness.

Someone Else's Dream

Your dream come true was actually someone else's dream for you. There is someone near and dear to us who hasn't lived out his or her dreams and they have imparted their dream to us. This is common with parents. They use their children to live out the dreams they did not accomplish. Dive deeply into your heart to discover your true dreams. Our most powerful dreams express who we uniquely are; and are not about pleasing other people!

This is why in Chapter 1 I said it takes real courage for real dreaming. If you identify that a dream you thought was yours is actually someone else's, great news! You can go back to Step One to discover your *true desires;* and start afresh with your *true dream statement! Now that's real progress!*

Vague Visualization

I tend to dream in big pictures because I am not adept at visualizing details. Once the bigger picture starts to form, I can begin to see the details I want with more clarity. It is then a matter of creating a secondary dream to fill in the details!

We have the home of our dreams, but the home requires too much maintenance for us to enjoy. The dream for a spacious home was fabulous except it is difficult to keep it warm.

To adjust a detail in the dream that isn't completely to your liking, start all over at step one in your dream imagination to create a new "sub-dream."

For example, if your home requires too much maintenance to enjoy, create a new dream to augment the story of the base dream. Dream for a gardener, manager, maintenance person whose dream is to live and work on your property full time.

Limiting Beliefs Block Parts of the Dream

Our dream come true arrives, but a piece of it is not quite right. Deep in our subconscious and deeper in our nervous system and biochemistry is a stubborn core belief. It won't allow the completion of your dream-come-true. Examine the unsatisfactory part of your dream. Your subconscious will speak in picture code to your consciousness and will point to the limiting belief preventing what you desire in your heart.

If you are challenged by part of the dream that's not coming true, go back for a Power Study on limiting core beliefs. Beliefs are the stage for our dream dramas to play on. If our stage is too small, we need to restructure our belief systems to provide a bigger stage on which our dreams may better perform.

Receive the Dream with Thankfulness

Remind yourself to be thankful for your dream come true, and continue practicing thankfulness on a daily basis. If you have not developed this habit, your dream come true will not excite your life. Without thankfulness, you will not fully receive the dream. You will block its fulfillment and its enjoyment as well.

Goldilocks and the Three Bears

Dreams that come true are among the most exciting, fulfilling experiences in life! However, sometimes they go a lot easier in the mind than when they enter reality. Make adjustments and allow yourself some time to make the dream fit just right. Sometimes we get a chance to try on a dream! If you get that chance, accept it fully, or change it a little, or even a lot. This gives you the opportunity to see if they are truly your own dreams, and if the details are just as we want them.

Authoring Your Reality is an ongoing process and takes time. Remember "Goldilocks and the Three Bears"? Perhaps you recall the story about a little girl trespassing in a home that wasn't hers. It is my thought that she was practicing her dreaming, and she was dreaming big and bravely!

Take a hint from *Goldilocks*. Try out a few things—some might be too big or too small, some might be too hot or too cold, others might be too hard or too soft. Allow yourself the luxury of "trying your dream on" until it's "just right!"

KEY POINTS TO REMEMBER

1. *Authoring Your Reality* is a skill set that can be developed.
2. Dreaming takes practice and adjustments.
3. Find out what adjustments need to be made.
4. Practice thankfulness for dreams that have come true.
5. Create sub-dreams to perfect your dreams.

POWER STUDY ABOUT POWER OF ATTRACTION

The Secret is a documentary movie proving the idea of the power of attraction. Our inner thoughts and subsequent actions attract the elements of our personal outer world.

Website: www.thesecret.tv

FINAL
ACHIEVE

Chapter 16

Become a Dream Achiever

> "I have a dream that my four children will one day live in a nation where they will not be judged by the color of their skin but by the content of their character."
>
> –Martin Luther King, Jr.

Now Dream Big

AT THE BEGINNING of this book, and throughout the companion workbook, we asked you to start with small dreams to learn the skill set of *authoring your reality*. Small successes create confidence, and confidence creates momentum. Once you have learned the dream steps and personalized them as your own, you may now create even bigger dreams.

Become a Dream Achiever

As I complete the writing of this book, Barack Obama is the first African-American President of the United States of America. I reflect on the larger dream that started playing on the American stage 40 years ago.

Martin Luther King had a dream. That dream was larger than Martin Luther King. It was so big that it reached into this "now" and has affected all of mankind.

Modern day quantum physics has substantial evidence that "the observer," (dream implementer) affects the substance being observed. This means we have power to affect the world around us in minor and major ways.

Perfect the *author your reality* method starting with your smaller personal dreams. Then graduate to bigger dreams. Take your dreams to all the interspaces of the universe to create a better world all around you. Become a dream achiever to create unlimited dream wealth.

It's a Wonderful Life

One of the most visible examples of personal influence is the premise of the movie *It's a Wonderful Life*. Jimmy Stewart, the leading man, has a number of impossible challenges that seem to undermine the very fabric of his entire existence. He has lived a life of service and sacrifice, giving and loving in a most unselfish way. Yet selfish players all around him attempt to viciously steal everything that is precious to him.

Distraught by a seemingly impossible situation, he attempts suicide. Instead, he is rescued by an angel who gives him a magical gift. The gift is that of showing him how the microcosm around him would have been if he had never been born. The angel replays his life for him as if it is a play, but his character is left out of the script!

Everything is different and a whole lot worse for all those he knew and loved. All the good things he has done in his life were voided, and the consequences were far reaching. This movie beautifully demonstrates the concept that each of us influences the micro-world that surrounds us.

Back to the Future

Back to the Future was an intriguing movie that used a time machine to prove the same idea. The key character actually goes back to the past and recreates the future in a positive way by encouraging his father to make better choices! The title, *Back to the Future,* paints the picture that time is an interpretation of the possibilities created by our choices. This same point is being proven in modern quantum physics and documented in the movie, *What the Bleep Do We Know?* If you aren't the cerebral type, the movie *Back to The Future* tells the story in a very kinesthetic way! It clearly shows us how actions taken in moving towards our dreams and desires can change our world—past, present, and future.

Big Brave Dream Achievers

The power of bigger dreaming and achieving those dreams is the power to inspire. Without leaders and dreamers and "without a vision, the people perish." (The Bible: Proverbs 29:18).

Martin Luther was another big dreamer. His dream was to make the Bible available to the common man through his translation of the Bible into the vernacular of the people; and had a tremendous political impact on the church. His dream created the beginning of an entire religious sect called "Protestantism," an alternative to the one authoritative religion of his day, Catholicism.

The founders of our country were big dreamers. Benjamin Franklin, Thomas Jefferson, and George Washington framed the American Dream for us. Most of our grandparents were big dream achievers. They left their homeland and came to the United States to engage in the big dream of freedom and opportunity. They crossed an ocean and endured the hardships of learning a new language, acquiring a new home, and a new vocation. It takes courage to identify a dream; then to admit the dream, to plan and take the action required to live it out.

Great American Dream

The people who left England and those who left the Eastern United States to move west were big dreamers. They moved slowly across the land in wagon trains to start new lives, to settle new towns, and to find gold. Their dreams came true. They found gold and settled the Western United States.

Shoot for the Moon

"One small step for man, one giant leap for mankind." These were the first words spoken by Neil Armstrong in 1969 as he took his first steps on the moon.

"I believe that this nation should commit itself to achieving the goal, before the decade is out, of landing a man on the moon and returning him safely to the earth. But . . . it will not be one man going to the moon—it will be an entire nation. For all of us must work to put him there."

This was the dream of President John F. Kennedy, who dared to dream big enough to include the entire country in this dream come true. What a great dream it was, too!

Once you strengthen your dream muscles, take your dreaming and your dream achievements to the next level. Be as courageous as all those who have gone before you . . . and don't forget to shoot for the moon—and the stars!

Ten Author Your Reality Steps

PART ONE: CONCEIVE

—**Step 1** Launch Your Courage
—**Step 2** Drive Your Desire
—**Step 3** Free Your Imagination

PART TWO: BELIEVE

—**Step 4** Stage Your Dream
—**Step 5** Pen Your Dream Script
—**Step 6** Set Your Dream on Fire

PART THREE: RECEIVE

—**Step 7** Publish Your Vision Book
—**Step 8** Inspire Your Dream with Action
—**Step 9** Awaken Your Dream with Thanks

FINAL: ACHIEVE

—**Step 10** Become a Dream Achiever

Dictionary of Terms

Dreaming Muscles: The idea that the *author your reality* concept can be learned and developed as a skill; and strengthened with use and practice to conceive, believe, receive, and achieve a dream on purpose.

Author Your Reality Process: The on-purpose process, from beginning to end, that propels its creator through conceiving, believing, receiving, and achieving a dream objective.

Dream Deniers: Those emotions, obstacles, and persons who would try to separate dreams from the manifestation of their dreams.

Dream Doers: Those persons who are determined to follow their dreams and make them come true!

Dream Elements: Creative graphic pieces of meaningful artwork, personal photos, quotes, thoughts, words, poetry, designs, colors, shapes, and scanned images brought together to tell the dream story in a *published vision book*.

Dream Achiever: A dream achiever is an advanced and practiced dream writer able to dream dreams so powerful that they reach beyond their own lives and times, to create dream wealth for others.

Dream Objective: A passionately desired outcome.

Author Your Reality Action Plan: Includes three parts: introduction to dream planning, interactive online workbook, and use of proprietary software for creating a self-published dream plan.

Dream Script: As Dream writers, we become the author of our dreams. We deliberately write a story line from which to build our dream stories, which ultimately become our published dream plans.

Dream Statement: A simple explanation in 15 words or less, defining a vision, goal, or idea that one has decided to conceive, believe, receive, and achieve. This statement forms the basis of the dream script.

Dream Story: The narrative that a dream writer creates in preparation for writing their *published vision book.*

Published Vision Book: The physical outcome of the *Author Your Reality Action Plan.* It is a 7"x 7" 10 to 40-page book, authored by the reader in the simple format of a children's book. It is the dream writer's illustrated, creative narrative of their defined deliberate dream objective.

Dream Theme: It is the emotional component, which emerges from the dream script to form a dream storyline.

Dream Wealth: A concept coined by author of *Author Your Reality* to refer to the unlimited abundance expressed by the soul when united with its source.

Dream Writer: A dream writer is a deliberate dreamer who creates a dream statement, script, and story to become the author of his/her own person *published vision book.*

Dream Objective: A passionately desired outcome.

Powerful Resources

AngelArts: Dana Susan Beasley, graphic artist, publisher, writer, entrepreneur. Websites: www.anqelarts.biz, www.anqelartswebstore.com.

The Bible: The scripture quotes of Jesus Christ can be found in the New Testament of the *Holy Bible*.

Creative Visualization, by Shakti Gawain: This is a simple and powerful book on how to activate the power of imagination and visualization in a purposeful way. Website: www.shaktiqawain.com.

Do what you Love, the Money Will Follow: Marsha Sinetar, 1989, Random House. Website: www.marshasinetar.com.

Magnificent Mind at Any Age, Dr Daniel Amen: A book about brain health and natural and preventative steps we can take to keep our brains healthy and energetic. Website: www.amenclinics.com.

Jamie Nelson Studios: Jamie Nelson, Fashion and Beauty Photographer. Website: www.iamienelson.com.

Power vs. Force, the Hidden Determinants of Human Behavior, by Dr. David Hawkins, MD., PhD: His research correlates vibration frequency measurements with states of mind and emotion. Website: www.veritaspub.com.

Psycho-Pictography: The new way to use the Miracle Power of Your Mind, By Vernon Howard: 1965 by Parker Publishing Company, Inc. Author uses the power of word stories and parable visualization to teach the some of the ages' greatest wisdom.

Pre-Paid Legal Services: Legal membership/insurance, and New York Stock Exchange Company, and business opportunity. Website: www.gcundiff.legalshield.com

Seaside Creative Services: Gwen Ellis, Editor, Author, Speaker. Website: www.seasidecreativeservices.com

Secrets of Manifesting: Paul Bauer, Dreams Alive, Website: www.dreamsalive.com.

The Astonishing Power of Gratitude, by Wes Hooper: There is a free PDF download of book at the website, www.dailygratitude.com. This book explains the power of gratitude goes beyond a spiritual principle, as it will also attract things of tremendous value into your life.

The Power of Intention, by Dr. Wayne W. Dyer, Hay House, Inc., Carlsbad, California, This book is about harnessing the power of what you strongly desire to bring it into reality.
Website: www.drwaynedyer.com.

The Power of Now, by Eckhart Tolle; 1999, Namaste Publishing. This book teaches the incredible power of the present moment, and gives ways to overcome the habit of living in the past and projecting fears into the future. Website: www.eckharttolle.com.

The Science of Getting Rich, by Wallace D. Wattles: Originally published 1910, free PDF download at website, www.scienceofgettingrich.net.

The Theory of Reality: Learn Quickly and Easily How to Change Your Life and Live Your Dream! By Larry and Diana Bogartz:

published by Xlibris Corporation. This is a book about faith as it relates to reality written from a scientific view. Included are great techniques for building and practicing faith.
Website: www.theoryofreality.com.

The Secret: A unique, independent documentary film addressing the idea that we attract that which we focus on.
Website: www.thesecret.tv.

The Way They Learn, by Cynthia Ulrich Tobias, Focus on the Family Publishing, 1998. An informative book which addresses the unique learning styles of different types of personalities.
Website: www.applest.com.

The Wizard of Oz, by Frank Baum (1939). A film starring Judy Garland, about ordinary people who go on a journey from wishing to dreaming, to living their dream; they ultimately take responsibility for their desires and dreams.

What the Bleep Do We Know? Down the Rabbit Hole: A documentary of interviews with scientists and Spiritualists involved in the research of quantum physics and where reality/perception meets up with physics. Website: www.whatthebleep.com.

www.AuthorYourDreams.com: website for Dream-writers, who intend to become the author and planner of their dreams; by writing their own personal *Published Vision Book*. It is a website of resources for the *Author Your Reality Action Plan.*

About the Author

Photography by Iamie Nelson

*D*REAMING AND WRITING—What do they have in common? Perhaps it is Deborah S. Nelson—who has united her two greatest talents within her recent book series, *Author Your Reality ACTION PLAN.*

Her ability to guide dreams to reality inspired Ms. Nelson to invent and author this unique three-part learning series—the first of its kind!

The author's first big dream, at 14, was to become a newspaper editor and writer. And she fulfilled that dream early on, within her first year of junior high school.

Her next dream was to fund her college education. Still in love with writing, between studies and work she made time to write for her college newspaper. Dreaming and writing, she graduated in the 70s, debt free, with a BS from the University of Texas. Soon after, she joined *The Austin Sun,* a weekly entertainment and cultural magazine.

In the '80s, Ms. Nelson emerged from a difficult divorce in the role of *sole functioning parent.* This challenge created just one thing for Nelson, a new dream—to raise her daughter as a happy, healthy, successful person, rather than as another statistic of a broken home.

Concern for her child's future propelled her into a new era and a new dream-to start one of the first "home-based businesses." That dream realized gave her freedom to be a full-time, *on-purpose, solo mom.*

Eventually, Nelson was able to fund most of her daughter's education at Brooks Institute of Photography, her daughter's dream college!

Devoted to women in business, Nelson was recognized by *Working Women Magazine* in the '90s for entrepreneurial excellence; and selected as a national finalist for Ms. Corporate America 2008—another childhood dream realized. In 2013, Nelson was nominated for the THE AMERICAN RIVIERA WOMAN ENTREPRENEUR OF THE YEAR, with a focus to celebrate woman change agents globally. As Nelson seeks to infiltrate the globe with dream doers, this is her most exciting recognition to date.

In the *Author Your Reality Action Plan,* a synthesis of 25 years of study, reading, and life experience, Nelson masterfully merges two recurring themes—her love of writing, and her ability to set dreams in motion. What is her next big dream? Her dream is to teach millions of readers how to write and publish their dream book and bring their dreams to reality!

Other Books by Deborah S. Nelson
Part II: The Newest Secret: The Author Your Reality Workbooks

Coming Soon!

Other Inspired Living Books

www.TheFreshFoodChef.com

www.DaretoDetoxify.com   www.TheRippleEffectGame.com   www.SuzanneLandry.com

www.ingramcontent.com/pod-product-compliance
Lightning Source LLC
Chambersburg PA
CBHW060159050426
42446CB00013B/2897